TWO BY MARK J. CURRAN

ASU Days
The Guitars - A Music Odyssey

Order this book online at www.trafford.com
or email orders@trafford.com

Most Trafford titles are also available at major online book retailers.

Print information available on the last page.

ISBN: 978-1-6987-1312-0 (sc)
ISBN: 978-1-6987-1313-7 (e)

Trafford rev. 10/11/2022

Trafford PUBLISHING® www.trafford.com
North America & international
toll-free: 844-688-6899 (USA & Canada)
fax: 812 355 4082

BOOK ONE
ASU DAYS

THE PH.D., THE FARM INTERVAL, BACHELOR DAYS, LIFE IN ARIZONA

Mark J. Curran

TABLE OF CONTENTS

PART II

INTRODUCTION

Two of my book titles refer to the "ingenuous" or "naïve" "gringo" in Latin America, so why not at home as well? The Ph.D. was in Spanish and Latin American Studies with a minor in Luso-Brazilian Studies. There are times now and even in the recent past when I asked myself, "Why did you pick this field? An Irish American boy raised on a wheat farm in Kansas teaching 'Don Quixote' or Jorge Amado's 'Gabriela Clove and Cinnamon?'" There has got to be a disconnect here. The short answer was I was unhandy, a klutz at Math and Science, loved living and growing up on the farm but having no idea how to run one, but from the beginning did well in language study, debate, history and the like. (I never did have a penchant for Literary Theory and that created some bumps in the road). I loved Spanish and had an incessant curiosity about the peoples and countries where it was spoken. And Brazil seemed the most exotic place with the coolest language I had ever experienced. And not so coincidentally they were all Catholic. (One can see a lot more about this in "Coming of Age with the Jesuits.") So, there you have it, a Ph.D. and off you go. You must proceed as best you can. Make the best of it!

Secondly, why Arizona State University? It was a thriving university in Tempe, Arizona, in a growth mode, some 24,000 students in the fall of 1968. The original "Normal School" for young, female teachers in 1885 reached university status only after an exceptionally difficult grassroots campaign by the students themselves and with the assistance of a successful football program under Dan Divine and then Frank Kush in the mid-1960s. Before that it was Arizona State College in Tempe, Arizona.

The University of Arizona in Tucson was the land grant school with a medical school and law school; the latter contributed many folks to the state legislature and tried to block the ASU move from State College to University status. But there were other components: ASU was known as one of the biggest party schools in the nation with a terrific climate, nice campus, and beautiful coeds. And it also in 1968 had one of the top track and field teams in the nation, its athletes in the Olympics and world record holders. And ASU football and baseball were on the rise.

Somewhere I already mentioned the reasons for my choice of Arizona State University related to Spanish: the proximity to Mexico, the Latin American Center, a new Ph.D. program in Spanish, but also the climate, the sports scene, and Spring Training Major League Baseball. There would be serious ramifications later for this choice when applying for national research grants. I daresay I never could compete, at least most of the time, in "grantsmanship" with colleagues from the Ivy League or the high-toned places like Stanford or Berkeley in the West (the selection committees were largely comprised of people from such places). I did compete in many other ways as it turned out. It all came out okay. See my web site: www. currancordelconnection.com. I'll gradually say more about this atmosphere at ASU after I tell of the road to get there.

PART I

A

CHICAGO, THE MLA, AND THE "MEAT MARKET" 1967

During an icy winter of 1967 good friend Dan Hayes from graduate school days at Saint Louis University drove me from St. Louis to Chicago to attend the Modern Language Association "Meat Market." Months earlier I had sent letters to those universities where I thought I might like to teach. I did this without a whole lot of research, the main factors being THE PLACE I would like to LIVE. It's been so long ago that I don't recall all the places, but I think of Tulane U., Kansas University, U. of Nebraska, and most importantly U. of Arizona in Tucson and Arizona State University in Tempe. I did not aim higher (just as when applying to graduate school) for the Ivy Leagues or big-time west coast schools. It was not that I did not have the confidence to be at such schools (the research year in Brazil on a Fulbright-Hays Graduate Fellowship and the competition and company I kept there easily showed me I could hold my own with such folks). My requirement was that the school would have a Latin American Studies Center and a respectable offering of Spanish and Portuguese. But there were other factors; U of A and ASU were both close to the border and I intended to spend a lot of time in Mexico. I loved athletics and ASU had some fine programs at the time. And Tempe had spring training. The weather and the campuses were beautiful. U of A was more prestigious and offered me a one-year contract but with no promises for tenure track the following year.

Nebraska had a Latin American Studies Center with a small press, and it would be close to home and relatives. But Dr. Van Scoy of the Department of Foreign Languages at ASU outbid them by $200 so we shook hands to "seal the deal." A formal offer, which may seem strange now, was in the form of a Western Union Telegram which I still have as a souvenir. The job was tenure track.

So, after the interviews in Chicago and a stay at the less than upscale LaSalle Hotel near the loop we piled back in Dan's car and drove through one of those major Mid-West ice storms with all the power lines coated with the stuff, plus I had a whopping case of the flu. So, Dan got me to the Union Pacific Railway Station in St. Louis, and I climbed aboard the passenger train for home and respite in Abilene. It was wintry; I was so sick; my Dad met me at the train and took us to the warm house on Rogers St. As I wrote another time, this was the last time I truly felt dependent on my parents at least in a material way, and it taught me a lot about parenting.

B

THE ODYSSEY NOT OVER AND THE STUFF HITS THE FAN

The odyssey was not over. I would spend the next four months living in the upstairs "loft" at Mom and Dad's house on Rogers Street in Abilene near Eisenhower Park, cubby holed at a desk with a Smith Corona typewriter trying to finish the formidable dissertation. All did not go smoothly. I had sent the first two chapters by mail to Father Rosario Mazza my Ph.D. advisor at Saint Louis University before the MLA convention, and there were many corrections. But then for some reason a new advisor came aboard, a truly scholarly Ph.D. with a bent for Literary Criticism. He basically wanted me to start over and do a "critical" study of the "cordel." I balked, taking the stance that both my style and the subject matter were much more attuned to a folkloric, journalistic or history approach, and made the mistake of writing that the new advisor was "pedantic." The manure hit the fan; Father Mazza was ready to throw me out of the program and right now! I'm not sure how things progressed, but the literary critic of course resigned from the case (who can blame him?), and Father Mazza was left holding the bag. I did manage to write two more short chapters, all was approved, great friend Jeannie Giese of M.A. English fame typed it, and finally it was approved. The main thing I found was that I did not have that much to say (scholars commented on this when it came out in a short book years later in Brazil), a contrast to the few thousand pages written and published now.

C

RETURN TO ST. LOUIS, GRADUATION AND THE FINAL DAYS

So, although I was actually awarded the degree in June of 1968, it was required for all candidates to be in person for graduation, so I returned to St. Louis and the university in the winter of 1968-1969, donned cap and gown, and actually received the diploma. It was at this juncture that Miss Keah Runshang really enters the picture, but that is another matter; family is private and will remain so.

Returning to that spring of 1968 prior to the awarding of the degree in June and the graduation the next winter, after perhaps two or three trips to St. Louis to deal with the finalities of the dissertation, bunking in Dan Hayes' parents' house in Maplewood where I spent probably the two most entertaining months of laughter of my life before or since, things were concluded. A tiny and very unpleasant part of this chapter was my trying to make just a few bucks by substitute teaching in the St. Louis city school system. It was not fun and there were some harrowing moments. The one time I did get to teach Spanish has always remained with me: when I walked into the classroom the students seemed to flash brilliance in conversation including excellent pronunciation. It turns out once they had completed their memorized dialogues, they could do nothing with the language. The text was the famous/ infamous "Modern Spanish" of the MLA based on dialogues and memorization. I would use the text some at ASU but greatly modified.

The Outing on "The Admiral;" The New Tatoo, and the Last Time with the Group

The Arch. St. Louis

The Friends on the Admiral

It's a foggy memory now, but I think the last outing in St. Louis was on the tour boat "The Admiral" which offered a ride down the Mississippi from St. Louis for about an hour and then back. We quaffed a few beers; earlier in the day Dan got his latest tattoo - the Owl symbolizing Minerva Goddess of Wisdom and flexed his muscles to show us. Jeannie Giese, Jo Anne and Tori Cusack, and Miss Keah Runshang and a couple of others were along. It was great fun for all.

So, I drove home to Abilene after getting the final approval of the dissertation, the manuscript now soundly ensconced in a Xerox paper box.

D

Return to the Farm in Abilene, but Now with Ph.D. in Hand

I do not know if it was by plan, but an opportunity arose for the three months before departure to Tempe for my first (and it turned out last) teaching job. Good friend Gordon Kippenberger, with the death of his Dad Joe, was now farming all the family land which included rented land down on the Smokey Hill River, the original Kippenberger farm east and south of Brady Street near the old Municipal Hospital, and Gordon's home place several miles north of Abilene. He needed summertime help and I filled the bill. Perhaps it is good to recall that Gordon's brother Mike was my best friend growing up in Abilene in the 1940s and 1950s, many of our adventures accounted in the book "The Farm." Gordon shared a love for the old Hank Williams songs and could even play a few ditties on the guitar; I think I taught him more.

So, we were together at least six days a week for close to three months. It was a true "coming home" experience and aside from earning just a fair amount of cash, it mainly got the intellectual cobwebs out of my head and body and got me a little back in physical shape prior to the new life in Arizona. All was not health and sunshine; we both smoked cigarettes at work while riding the huge farm tractors or even the wheat harvester. And I had a small inconvenient moment: with all the land involved, a fair amount of transporting machinery from one farm to another took place. Most of the time you simply drove the big tractor down the country and county byways to the next place. I got to drive the John Deer Dually (dual tires on the rear) many times. In this case we were unloading the tractor and a huge wing – disk in the barnyard. The wing sectors of the disk are propped up for travel. In letting them down, one came a little too fast and leveled a blow to my middle right toe. Luckily the toe was just broken but not severed. The next day I bought an extra heavy pair of work boots, taped the big and middle toes together and hobbled off to work. In passing, an old mantra from growing up on the farm (borrowed from artist Gary Larson), I was totally "mechanically declined," but in one sense it was a good thing because I was extra cautious around the machinery and had the standing record, at least, of not breaking equipment. This is no small thing in farming.

It's been so many years, but I recall the dust and dirt on the tractor in the field whether disking, plowing or whatever (Gordon did not have the air-conditioned tractor cab that would come in later years for most successful farmers). And of course, there was the Kansas heat and humidity. And we baled hay still much in the old style of my Dad's time: one man on the hayrack grabbing the bale ejected from the back end of the bailer and stacking it, another person on the tractor. It must have been this time when we exchanged some work with my brother-in-law Johnny Whitehair and his brother Dick Whitehair on bottom land south of town. I can recall being on the rack and trying to lift the 80-pound alfalfa bales and stack them ideally four rows high. I simply was not strong enough to get beyond two rows and was close to collapse in that intense Kansas heat and humidity and hot sun. Johnny laughed, never let me forget it, but he was not mean about it.

Because Gordon's wife Joyce worked full-time at a local Abilene bank, lunch time was not the old-style big farm meal cooked by the wives, but rather a decent lunch at a working man's café on the south side of Abilene, what used to be the old "A Street," infamous for cowboy bars and houses of prostitution. You got the "blue plate" special with iced tea and probably a piece of pie for dessert. And then it was back out to the machinery.

All Was Not Work

I'm trying to recall what I did for socializing that summer; the girlfriend of years back when I was working at the Abilene Ice Plant in summers between academic years at Rockhurst College in Kansas City, Missouri, was a thing of the past. I do know that Howie's Tavern on Third Street in Abilene with the icy Coors beer on tap was still a gathering place. I think the ten-cent glass of beer was now perhaps a quarter, but there were a few of the old high school buddies and local farm buddies in the joint. And I know one night Bob Hensley, Eddy Smith and I did some music in the bar and later in front of the band shell in Eisenhower Park. On one occasion Mike and Jack Kippenberger joined us and the night was full of Hank Williams' "Whippoorwill" and other songs. The police would drive by, but we were not making any trouble, so all went well.

In sum, I do not know what Gordon and I talked about throughout all that time that summer, but we talked constantly, joked and laughed a lot. I'm sure I was not talking about Spanish Golden Age Literature or the Brazilian Novel. But I can say now in this narrative "Thank you Gordon." It was truly "mission accomplished" with some help for him and a healthy summer for me. And it was the last meaningful work experience on a farm since then. It was time to move on.

Note: in late 2021 I saw the "Abilene Reflector Chronicle" online and there was the obituary of Gordon Kippenberger with a fine photo. I saved it and eventually wrote to sister Betty Kippenberger Krenger expressing my condolences.

Gordon Kippenberger, the Farm

E

The Move to Tempe, Arizona, September 1968, and a New Life

1. TRANSPORTATION

I probably had just a few hundred dollars to my name that early September in 1968. Transportation was the old black 1963 Chrysler 300 inherited from my brother Jim. It was gathering dust and rust in a garage on my sister Jo and Johnny Whitehair's farm, the victim of yet another of Jim's beer drinking and carousing nights in central Kansas. One entire side was entirely bashed in, but the other was perfect, so it became a matter of perspective and or luck as you might drive down Main Street. The inside however was luxurious for the times. It would take me to Arizona, not readily, but eventually until just a year and one half later a nice modest but shiny Chevrolet Malibu would enter the scene as did Keah Runshang.

The car however was jammed full of my bachelor possessions: a few sports coats and slacks and clothes from college days, the Smith Corona typewriter, many heavy LPs of a growing music collection (The Kingston Trio, the Limelighters and Nonesuch Classical) and of course my Di Giorgio Classic Guitar purchased in Brazil in 1966, my "first love" I used to say, certainly the most valuable possession.

Other items were the boxes of books from school days and more importantly the boxes with many file folders of the precious notes taken in all the graduate classes. These I would use to the utmost over the years in preparing classes at ASU.

It all made for a full automobile probably running on well - worn or even bald tires and an altogether unreliable motor.

The main goodbye was to Mom and Dad on the house in Rogers. Strangely enough I don't recall details, but that the main thing was them wishing me well in that new life and promises on my part to always write and visit on the holidays.

2. AN ASIDE IMPORTANT FOR THE FUTURE

Perhaps one of the revealing moments of this book of life and customs has been touched on here. The "letter home" to Mom and Dad, once a week, from the first days of separation while at school at Rockhurst College in Kansas City and then Saint Louis University in St. Louis, and the entire year from Brazil, but then on-going until their death was a component of our relationship (I daresay it continued with Keah years later.) I was always out-going, successful as a leader at school, a leader on our state prize winning high school debate team, and of course a language teacher five days a week for forty years. So, I could talk with the best of them. (Where am I going with this?) I am notoriously to the point in a telephone conversation "I go now"), did the requisite phone calls over the years, but was much more comfortable writing a letter and later an email.

There's more. I'm jumping ahead but it is apropos. After marrying Keah and beginning our lives and later the huge experience with daughter Katie, there would be a weekly call with Mom and Dad in Abilene, and certainly with George and Ginni on Keah's side of the family. When Mom and Dad died, something happened, something changed. It's been so long ago, but I am sure I tried to keep up weekly letters with Jo Anne in Abilene. So, to make a long story short, I use the phone infrequently and in short talks. (Notwithstanding I handled a 45-minute telephone interview with Jen Martin of Lindblad-National Geographic in 2013.) Slight deafness and hearing aids have added a new chapter to the telephone.

All this was to explain my goodbye to Mom and Dad and the letters to follow.

3. THE TRIP TO ARIZONA AND THE ARRIVAL IN TEMPE

I'm sure I had it all planned and mapped out. Without looking at a map now, the route probably was cutting south through the Oklahoma Panhandle, then the Texas Panhandle, across New Mexico and then eventually down the Mogollon Rim to the Salt River Canyon, through the mining towns of Miami and Globe and their notorious smelters at the time and on into the east valley of Phoenix on US 40.

Whatever the route, the first breakdown took place in Garland, Texas (early September 1968), and had something to do with the radiator or radiator hoses. It got it fixed for about $45 and I was on my way.

The only other memory was in early September coming into the Salt River Valley of Phoenix from the east, over that last rise at Globe or Miami and the horizon was white hot! The Chrysler 300 did not have a working air conditioner. At any rate after dropping down to highway 60 I drove for what seemed like hours in that infernal heat along the old Apache Trail through east Mesa and finally, exhausted, spent the first night in a motel not yet arriving in Tempe!

4. THE FIRST "DIGS" AND A LASTING FRIENDSHIP

A Lasting Friendship, Philip and Mary

Through the classifieds, I found an ad from some guys wanting a roommate to help split the rent on one of those modest college apartments in an apartment complex in "Sin City" just east of the ASU campus. Few memories of that remain, but there is one: one night I came home after several beers in Frank's Friendly Tavern, and they tried to convert me to Mormonism. I guess the need was obvious to them. Not wanting anything to do with that, I moved out shortly and got my own studio apartment I think in the same complex. Once a Catholic, …

What did provide a great moment happened in those days before classes started at ASU. The novelty of the apartment complex was its swimming pool, ubiquitous in those parts. So, I was swimming and sunning by the pool and struck up a conversation with a fellow who turned out to be like me, a first-year professor at ASU. This was Philip Leonard from Boston,

M.A., Ph.D. in Mathematics in Number Theory, married to his delightful wife from upstate Vermont but a coed from a Catholic Girls School in Boston. They had moved from Happy Valley and his degree program from Penn State. The moment was propitious and happy: the Leonards would become close, great friends in Tempe at ASU, and the friendship has lasted to the present day. They are, off and on, an important part of our lives.

I will write of many moments with them, then during the bachelor days, on a special trip with "friend" Keah and them to southern Arizona and socializing to the present. There is so much to tell, but among other things it was they who sponsored Keah and me on the Marriage Encounter Weekend probably in 1974 which would change all our lives.

5. THE DAY AND THE MOMENT – INTRODUCTION TO THE DEPARTMENT OF FOREIGN LANGUAGES

On one of those mornings, I donned sports coat, tie, white short sleeved shirt, and dress slacks, drove the perhaps two blocks to the ASU parking lot and presented myself on the fourth floor of the Language and Literature building of ASU. I appreciated the air conditioning but not the clothing; it soon was modified. There was a very cordial secretary who greeted me that day, one of the many Mormons employed in the Department; she welcomed me, gave me a key to my office not in the DLL but to what turned out to be a spacious and fine office in the new Mathematics Building east down the mall. Construction would augment the LL building from four floors to six within the next few years, and I would move once again to a spacious office on the fourth floor, joining the language crowd. Those perhaps three years in the Math Building were a blessing because it allowed me to meet professors with other interests, many whom would become good friends in Arizona, certainly Philip Leonard but then also Frank Farmer. I recall the coffee lounge where a non-mathematician was welcomed, and we seemed to find plenty to talk about.

6. BACK TO THE BEGINNINGS: SIN CITY, SOUTH STANLEY APARTMENTS, THE LEONARDS AND REGGIE JACKSON

Back to the apartment on S. Stanley, my first as a bachelor at ASU in 1968. I soon became friends with Philip and Mary Leonard on the ground floor of the apartment complex. There was a celebrity on the second floor, Reggie Jackson of ASU and now Oakland Athletics baseball fame. Reggie had smacked something like 47 home runs the previous season and was back at ASU off season to pick up the courses to get his college degree. His presence was noted because of a big, shiny, black luxury car with some type of wheel or tire locks that went off like a siren if you tampered with them. This happened more than once in the middle of the night on S. Stanley.

There was one other anecdote. Reggie needed an advanced math course to graduate, heard about Philip Leonard in the complex, and came for tutoring on Saturday mornings. Phil recounted one such session: Reggie was not "getting the concept," but in his defense told the Math teacher, "You probably can't get the hang of a baseball bat hitting a major-league pitcher's curve either. So, we're even." I do not know how the course turned out, but Philip and I did bet a case of Blatz Beer (returnable glass bottles with deposit, total value a little over $ 2.00) on how many homers Reggie would hit the following season. I was on the high side, so had to pay up.

Another anecdote as I think of it. Philip was now a married man, Mary expecting their first child in coming months, so he did not get to carouse like some of us bachelors. But we did have a celebratory night at a very nearby bar, famous in ASU lore: "The Library." I recall quaffing drafts at the bar and both of us not getting home in too good of shape. It was a one-time thing for us.

Any regular beer drinking for me took place at a tiny bar in an old house on Apache, all within walking distance of my apartment. Frank's Friendly Tavern was the place. It wasn't exactly "Cheers" of Boston fame, but it had a down home atmosphere, and you could get to know some people. The feature was the bar itself, a jukebox with lots of pop and country tunes, and one of those bowling machines you slid a "puck" down to knock down the pins. The place owed its fame as a watering hole of ASU coaches of those days, most notably Frank Kush the football coach.

Right across the street was the Buckhorn Café with its claim to fame in 1968: for 99 cents, you could get three eggs, three slices of bacon, three pancakes or toast, or potatoes and coffee. It eventually went by the way, maybe not keeping up with the economic times, but I and the Leonards, George Carver from Saint Louis University and classics teacher at ASU, and later Keah spent some good chow time up there on Sunday a.m.

George would drive me upon occasion to a lunch buffet at a place in one of the shopping centers in N. Tempe. I recall good roast beef and great conversations with the slow talking, almost drawl of the Texan who taught Classics at ASU. George will enter the story more as we go along.

7. THE PH.D. AND CLEANING THE APARTMENT BATHROOM

And since we leased our apartments in Sin City, you had to pay for nine months, September to May, I guess. I did find myself down on my knees one Saturday morning cleaning the toilet bowl. There was an "army" like inspection by the 'ole gal that ran the place in order to get your deposit back. But I was thinking, "I got a Ph.D. for this?" (Mary Leonard howled at this.) Unless one is of the ilk of those with hired help, the maid and the like, I learned this would become a lifelong chore. But back on that day in 1969 it was onerous. I think I was drinking a bottle or two of A-1 beer to get through it. The A-1 brewery was in downtown Phoenix, and I surmise this concoction was the worst beer at least west of the Mississippi, and maybe the cheapest. I know the total consumption was planned to be one six-pack, but I threw a few bottles out. I told Mary Leonard about my travail, and she laughed and laughed.

Mary would also remind me of my naïve, bachelor concerns on another occasion. She was about to "pop," giving birth to Andrew their first child. Philip, I believe, was away for a conference for the weekend so I was asked to "Keep an eye" on Mary in case she needed transportation to the hospital. I would call their apartment and say, "Mary, I'm going into the shower now, but I'll call right away when I get out." Mary heehawed over my concern but was grateful just the same. Our friendship has endured.

Yet another anecdote of the times was when we were socializing with the Leonards at a friend's apartment in Tempe and I had my guitar and was asked to play a classical selection or two. Both the Leonards and the hosting couple were from New England and were all a bit refined in their tastes and perhaps reserved as well. I managed to play some rather challenging and beautiful pieces, but before starting on one, commented for all to hear: "Let's ring the snot out of this one Jake." I think it was the Romero's "6 Lute Pieces of the Renaissance."

8. THE EARLY ASU ACADEMIC MOMENTS

A. THE PORTUGUESE PROGRAM AND DR. QUINO MARTINEZ

Although with a Ph.D. in Spanish and Latin American Studies, it was my work and preparation in Portuguese and Brazil that was the real reason for getting hired at ASU, so I'll start there: the Portuguese Program and early experience. I'll start by recalling that my beautiful office in the Math building was quite sufficient for giving what we called Reading and Conference courses to the graduate students. I recall that Louie Martínez came for something, perhaps a survey on Brazilian Literature. Louis was the son of my senior colleague Dr. Quino Martínez raised in Silver City, New Mexico, Ph.D. University of New Mexico, and of fame as a Peace Corps director in Recife, Brazil in the early 1960s. I'm sure Louis reported the pros and cons of my efforts to his Dad. The elder Martínez would enter my story many times over the coming years.

Quino was the senior professor in both Spanish and Portuguese and was set up to be my "boss" in matters of Portuguese. I was hired specifically by Dr. Van Scoy in Chicago to "help build up the Portuguese program" at ASU. So, would we mesh? His field was language and linguistics, and he was of the old school, teaching a priority over publishing, giving emphasis to his classes. Quino had chosen and ordered the Portuguese Text for POR 101 which would be my baptism of fire in that fall of 1968. The text (how could I forget?) was "Portuguese Grammar" by Father Rossi, S.J. It was a reference grammar, practically impossible to use to teach a beginning language course. But Quino knew I was coming from the Jesuits so maybe it was a favor. Anyway, it got changed out second year at ASU for something more manageable.

Quino was the "old guard" in the DFL and was in on important decisions in the future direction of the Department, i.e. the personnel committee and tenure decisions. But he was also "old school" in that he published rarely, and I do not think read many academic papers at conferences; this was just something not in the mix in the ASU of the early 1960s. It all would change with the arrival of David Foster in Spanish to build the Ph.D. program based on serious research, consistent and even "massive" publication and the like.

Not wanting to make waves, recalling I truly was a "rookie" and without tenure, I went out of my way to get along with Quino. We had a fifteen-minute meeting in his office (always his, he never came to mine except on one occasion or two, one asking my support in his quest to be department chair) to split up the teaching assignment in Portuguese for the semester. It was always the same and agreed with us both: I took the beginning 101 section or perhaps two sections, he did the 201 and the third level of composition and conversation. (That must have changed years later because I did the 313-314 upon occasion.) We rarely had enough students for a literature course until years later, but I think we switched off on that as well. Things went rather well for years. It was only much later that Carmello Virgillo from Spanish and Italian decided he wanted to return to Portuguese and eased his way into the pattern. And it was he who would bring in Ms. Clarice Deal, a Brazilian to help in the lower courses. By then I was a senior professor and was not so concerned about the lower division courses. And Clarice became a boon to the program. Today she has indeed carved her "niche" and does amazing things with on-line courses. We got along well.

I must add this "aside" about Carmelo. He was the quintessential Italian with personality to match. A marvelous language teacher with impeccable Italian (of course), Spanish, Portuguese, French and of course English. He could be fiery and feisty or outgoing and incredibly funny. Two anecdotes suffice: you had to be careful saying hello in the morning if you did not want his take on the world. "Bom dia! How are you?" Both were dangerous. A standard Virgillian reply: "If you think you got it bad, listen to what happened to me" (spoken in an Eastern accent from New York). The second was a brief encounter in his office shortly before he retired (I often went to his office for morning coffee and strategy, and he kept me posted on the many fights going on in the department). He simply said, "Mark I feel like a f****** dinosaur here." I think that was not far from my feelings in 2011 after the "part – time" retirement.

It was however in the beginning the first-year Portuguese language course that brought my most meaningful and fun times in those early days at ASU.

B. THE CLASSES – PORTUGUESE 101 AND 201

It's coming back now, and it is very interesting to know the rationale for this sequence. Quino had set up the courses in the school catalogue and had gone against the grain in doing so, but I totally agreed with his thinking. The concept is: the clear majority of students who would enroll in Portuguese would first have taken Spanish, and many were ethnically Hispanic. It is not a huge jump from Spanish to Portuguese, that is, if one applies oneself and if one has a bit of a gift for language. Therefore,

Quino set up POR 101 as the elementary course for 5 hours credit; POR 201 as the second-year course of 5 hours credit, and POR 313-314 Portuguese Conversation and Composition (3 credit hours each) as the third-year courses. (In effect skipping the standard rubric of 201 and 202, intermediate courses.) In the end the student would have sixteen hours credit roughly equivalent to two full years of Spanish, French, Latin, etc. instruction. It was the numbers and hours of the first – year courses that were different.

I would have in a good year perhaps 25 to 30 students in the 101, almost all proficient in Spanish. The course would combine careful presentation of grammar and structure, daily practice in writing to master each new verb tense or the like, but all done in Portuguese and much oral repetition along with a day in language lab. No need to go into details, but we had fun and I do believe I had a knack for making it all fun. But there were old fashioned techniques as well: the main one was the daily ten original sentences of written homework which all would put on the blackboard and we all together would correct. You may think a typical reaction would be, "So what?" And blow it off. But no one wants to be embarrassed when the prof or colleagues point out his/ her errors. It was indeed a terrific learning tool. There was some "group" work when they could try to talk to each other as well. Language lab was a bit monotonous repeating the oral patterns from the old reel to reel tapes (Can you believe Wollensak recorders from the dark ages?), but I spiced things up with the best of Brazilian music and its lyrics. They loved it. Doug Simmons and Paul Estes spent hours putting my Brazilian "Música Popular Brasileira" LPs first to reel to reel and then to cassette for the lab.

Memorable students: Connie Broughton, Terri Drew, Alan Sandomir, Roberto Froelich, Larry Johnson, and Jim Emery, among others. I apologize for not mentioning others. I made a critical mistake upon retirement, tossing all the old grade books, hence the names.

C. THE BRAZIL CLUB

The real innovation was the Brazil club. I was sponsor and started it all. It was not really a club at all, but a Friday noon get - together for pizza and beer at a local joint just off campus. It was at that session that the long-lasting friendships would evolve, and I mean between the students and not just the prof and the students. In a totally relaxed atmosphere, they could practice some Portuguese and eat pizza and have a beer or two. I recall that it was a "religious" practice for me to stay for about one hour and head home to Keah that afternoon. I only learned later that the kids, at least some of them, would perhaps close the bar in the wee morning hours that same day. What they did I cannot be responsible for, but I do know the friendships and bonds between them sometimes lasted long after college days.

A minor contribution on my part was the Brazil Club t-shirt, something in vogue at the time. Ours was yellow, had a design of Snoopy the Dog saying "Me dá um beijo eu falo Brasileiro." Give me a kiss (the design was "stolen" from a common design of Snoopy of the days) I speak Brazilian! But the saying was all ours and inspired by me. I must get technical for a moment: depending on where you live, most likely if the word "Portuguese" is mentioned it means Portuguese from Portugal. The fact of the matter is that Brazilian Portuguese then and now predominated in most universities in the U.S., save for New England and a part of California. The pronunciation is like night and day; I can only compare it in a loose analogy perhaps to the English in London and in Texas or California. We in no way wanted our club or our language to be joined or mixed up with the mother country. And to rest our case, the best example of what I was getting at is the "cool" sound of Brazilian Portuguese from the era of the Bossa Nova, Tom Jobin, and the MPB of the times.

D. MUSIC AND "SAMBA NOVO" AND CARNIVAL

In about 1975 or so all was serendipity with the Portuguese classes and the Friday Pizza gathering. Many names I now forget, but there was indeed one major figure related to Carnival, Alan Sandomir of West Phoenix. Alan had perhaps several motives to learn Portuguese, among them go to Rio and Copacabana and see those Brazilian chicks, but there was one more important reason to learn Portuguese; he was absolutely crazy over Brazilian Music and the Bossa Nova, so learning some language and more importantly the cool "bossa nova" pronunciation was essential to the task. I would only really appreciate this later upon a couple of occasions, but this kid was brainy, talented and a hard worker when it was something he loved. He organized a Brazilian Band, "Samba Novo," involving several others from the class, and it was a fine group. Alan was trained in classic guitar, could play Heitor Villa Lobos' selections as well as some fine Bach or Fernando Sor, but it was João Gilberto, Tom Jobim, Vinicius de Morais and Baden Powell that held his interest in those days. It all ended up involving the Portuguese program.

You cannot have a Brazilian Portuguese language program without doing Carnival! Most know it as the big Brazilian "blowout" just before the startof Lent. The "jeito" in those early days was that "unofficially" the party would be sponsored by the Brazil Club (there were campus rules for alcohol, age, etc. but originally it was 20 to drink beer). Some characters from the group found a student rental house, or maybe that's where they lived, bought a couple of kegs of beer, brought a big stereo system, charged a cheap admission, and Carnival party happened. It was an enormous success and they pulled it off for maybe two years. I was only "unofficially" involved but the Brazil Club was a "sponsor." I was nervous and sure we would all be hauled down to the hoosegow for one thing or another. That was maybe 1973. Times have indeed changed. I know the cops were called for noise on more than one occasion. There was a change in the Arizona drinking law, moving even beer to age 21, so that put a certain damper on the event. As I said, I was only on the fringe; it is to the students' credit that they kept the ole' prof. out of it.

The bottom line is it became a big annual thing and was eventually taken over by the "Brazil Club" of Phoenix or something of the sort, this club with many Brazilians living in the area. And there was a whole new crowd, basically "partyers", and few particularly interested in the esoterica of dedicated study to the Portuguese language or its literature or history. So, I, even indirectly, was off the hook! But during carnival week I did my best to celebrate Brazil and the event at ASU. We always had a showing of "Black Orpheus" ("Orféu Negro"), and I played carnival music in lab that week and showed slides and videos of the carnival parade. The students also got my annual "telling" of the 10 day pre-during-post carnival parties I did in Rio in 1967. I cannot understate how all that changed first in Brazil, then all over the world with "modern" days. I look back upon those early days with certain nostalgia and certainly a bit of relief.

One final note on Alan. He went on to become a pharmaceutical representative in of all places, Salt Lake, Utah. I met him for a beer on one or two occasions later. Memories are fragile, but I think that Allan set up and was the main DJ for a night of Brazilian music weekly on the radio in Salt Lake. He had a self-made audience: all those Mormon RMs who returned home jazzed up with Brazilian music and a mastery of Portuguese and daily "life" in Brazil but not much Brazilian "High Culture" – history, literature, economics, sociology, and certainly not folklore. Does the reader see a certain point of view here?

A cultural note. Alan is Jewish, and I know I recall times he perhaps was studying the Torah and Hebrew perhaps for a Bar Mitzvah. But I wondered later, how did this jive with sunset Friday evening and the Beer-Pizza gatherings on Friday at ASU? I think, like me, he bowed out early. I wish we could meet again; I hope life has treated him well. He is in the "top 5" of my favorite students of all time at ASU. I forgot: one of our great connections was a mutual appreciation of W.C. Fields and Groucho Marx!

E. "SELLING" PORTUGUESE ON THE MALL

In those early days to not only perhaps stimulate enrollment in Portuguese language courses, but to ensure their survival, one tactic was a table on the main mall directly across from the library (done through the auspices of the Brazil Club) when I would get student volunteers like Connie Broughton or Terry Drew or others, all dressed in the yellow club t-shirt to encourage enrollment in POR 101. Since we did not even have an official minor (I dealt for many frustrating years with the bureaucracy of the College of Liberal Arts and the catalogue committee), the only tactic was as "related field" for Spanish majors and the major drawing card that 101 and 201 totaled 10 hours of credit. My main memory of the few amongst thousands of students passing by, "I thought they spoke Spanish in Brazil." Case closed.

F. AN ASIDE: CLASSROOM TEACHING AND "THE BOSS" DR. HERBERT VAN SCOY

Professor Van Scoy was a throwback to those old days when "white" guys who loved languages could predominate in L and L departments (we had several others, and I would later be a good example, but now much in the minority). After my rather intense teaching methods in both Spanish and Portuguese became known, kindly Dr. Van Scoy called me into his office with a few sage words of advice: "Mark, you need to remember you are not teaching at a Jesuit University now." So, read between the lines.

9. THE FIRST YEAR AND SOME MISCELLEANA

A. THE "BLOND BOMBSHELL"

Being single and available with supposedly a bright future in front of me, I felt no compunction in asking out one of the TAs in the DFL, a cute, well - built and very intelligent chick working on her M.A. in Spanish. I had never dated a blond in my life and she met the stereotype. We went to a football game or two and I even got her to go for a drive up on the Mogollon Rim to see fall colors on the way to Payson. It might have been this drive that was the straw that broke the camel's back: we went in the wreck of the Chrysler. Oh well. I think she had far more ambitious goals than even a Ph.D. language and culture teacher. I understand she ended up with a commercial airline pilot. Flying high instead of low.

B. THE HOME ECONOMICS LADIES AND SHOWS AT GAMMAGE AUDITORIUM

Another less than stellar attempt at socializing was taking one of the great gal profs from Home Economics (a label long ago deleted to "Family Studies" or who knows what else now) to a show or two at ASU's Gammage Auditorium. I am almost positive it was with her that I saw the infamous Johnny Cash, June Carter and Marty Robbins show. Wow! As a terrific fan of all, I was astounded when the Arizona audience booed Marty Robbins (the introductory act) off the stage in their hurry to hear the Cashes. I was ashamed for all of us. It was a concert replete with all their hits. The socializing never became serious, but the home- economics prof was fun to be with and I hope it was vice- versa.

I partially repeat: the plans for Gammage by the way, the "Birthday Cake" or whatever they called the Avant - Garde building, were done by Frank Lloyd Wright (living in Phoenix at that time) for some Mid-Eastern Oil Sheik who ended up not liking the plans. So somehow it ended up on the ASU campus, a beautiful and indeed unusual building. It was all in one monotonous color, a sort of burnt orange: walls, outside pillars, huge interior curtains, seats, stage and all. I and wife Keah and friends would attend memorable concerts there later on, primarily in regard to Flamenco and Classic guitar.

C. LONELINESS AND FRANK'S FRIENDLY TAVERN

I've mentioned this place earlier but just want to say in a way it saved my social "skin" that first year in Arizona. After preparing classes and grading many papers in the tiny apartment I would repair to Franks' for perhaps two beers at most and just to see some human beings for conversation. This of course would all evolve when Keah and I were married and at ASU my second year.

D. PARKING AT ASU

The student population in September 1968, was 24,000 students, quite a respectable number. ASU was in a growth mode (partly the reason I and many other new faculty were hired on), but I daresay nothing like post 2002 and Dr. Michael Crow who has "redone" the university in a business model, operating like a corporation, and now on –line and with Starbucks to boot to more than 80,000 in 2015. Update: in Fall 2022 there are 80,000 students on the various campuses in the Phoenix area and 60,000 on -line! The growth mode meant many new parking lots and perhaps four - storied parking buildings. My choice in 1968 was a gravel lot immediately east of the Engineering Complex on the east side of campus, not more than three blocks from my apartment complex. It's crazy: I could have walked in the same time as driving, but what the hell! One year's parking at ASU in those years was, are you ready, $5.00 per either semester or year, anywhere! I recall a conference at UCLA and the then astronomical fee of $500 the San Fernando Valley Portuguese Professor was paying. ASU has caught up and perhaps surpassed that number. Does this mean it is now "big time?" Drive to the campus today and see what can happen to a pleasant, mid-sized university campus turned into a mega business.

This all affects me as an old-timer emotionally. But more importantly, imagine how the times have changed life for the students – I Pads, Cell Phones, on – line Education, Tuition doubled and doubled and doubled again. I cannot even begin to imagine; I am so out of the loop. It is good to be retired. So much of this narrative is now just ancient history.

E. THE BEAUTIFUL CAMPUS AND THE BEAUTIFUL CO - EDS

Let's tell it like it is. Even in 1968 ASU was known as the party school of the Southwest. I did **NOT** go there for that reason, I swear, but there were "residuals." Let's see: summer heat held on through October and the magic day when the temperature would drop below 100 degrees. Winter "heat" of mild 70 or even 80 degrees held through most of the winter. Late spring and the coming heat could begin in late April. So, what did the coeds wear?

Short skirts (remember the mini skirt?) or short shorts, or skintight jeans, and tight, revealing tops. After eating the sack lunch in my office, I might sidle out to the mall and just watch the scenery go by, I'm sure it was "good" for karma and digestion. My friend from Mathematics, Frank Farmer would join me upon occasion, just two innocents, ole' faculty guys taking the air.

Three perhaps significant changes took places over the years: 1. Bicycles ruled on the malls, you had to watch your step. 2. Cell phones were everywhere. I recall the minute the classroom bell rang, and the hundreds of students poured out of the Language and Literature Building; they all were on the phones. Keah and I still don't own a cell phone other than the emergency one we use in the car. I've wondered if it is because I don't have enough friends! I will attempt to re-create the last cell phone conversation I heard when wheeling my bicycle outside the L and L building for the last time when I retired. **SEX, SEX AND MORE SEX.** 3. The trend which was always a bit present at ASU although not the rule, became the rule around the time I retired: many of the coeds with all present low-cut blouse revealing enough "décolletage" or boobs, as it were, to make a healthy young man weak. I've always wondered how it is the young guys of today can face this front forward all the time and "be cool" and not notice.

Em fim, it's another world. The times they are a'changin.'

F. THE FIRST PAYCHECK AND THE VALLEY NATIONAL BANK

This was the Geodesic Dome "round bank" on Apache where I deposited my meager ASU check, retirement taken out and not much left. I happened to be there the first time with Charlie O'Bannon of Civil Engineering. His check was two or three times the size of mine. I think this was after mandatory retirement subtraction (a good thing; the state of Arizona matched my 7 per cent first for ASRS and then TIAA-CREF.) The first paycheck was for two weeks' work. I would collect every two weeks for 34 years, never missing a beat. I think I still may have the original stub but maybe not. The old geodesic dome was later demolished, first for parking, etc. Now it is the place of the ASU Honors College/ Prison ugly as it is.

Incidentally, with those first meager paychecks I paid back my $500 loan from Abilene National Bank for Mexico study and travel in 1962, but with about $500 in interest. Students with student loans today (and the last 20 years) would not believe this.

G. FALL, 1968, AN ICON OF THE TIMES AND AN ATTEMPT AT "BEING WITH IT"

Peter Jackson and the Training Jet

It turns out there were two or three other interesting moments in the bachelor year. A good friend, first of Keah's, then both of us in St. Louis, was young, handsome, debonair Peter Jackson who joined the Air Force and would be in flight school at the old Williams Air Force Base in east Mesa (now gone and converted into a feeder commercial airport for greater Phoenix). Peter was well on his way to graduating, having trained first in a prop trainer and then a single engine jet. The goal was to become a fighter pilot. I think that Peter for whatever reason was relegated to becoming trained in no less than the huge military transports, something akin to the Boeing 707 or larger. I know he flew those for a while, was it during Viet Nam Era? But also, that post service he became one of those private jet pilots you hear about, on call to haul rock bands and celebrities in their private "Lear" Jets or the like all over the nation.

Peter enters this time and place by giving me a call and saying he had membership in the Playboy Club in downtown Phoenix and would I like to go with him to check the place out? Are you kidding? Any red-blooded young man of that era would jump at the chance. So, we drove to Phoenix, checked it out, ogled the Bunnies for one night, and that was that. (There is some link to this and St. Louis. The Playboy Bunny Club was just a door or two down from Keah's apartment building on Lindell, and I think Peter was involved in that one too.)

Just a short aside but important for all this: the drive to Williams Airbase in 1968 was via Baseline Road in south Tempe. The entire drive for perhaps ten to fifteen miles was through agricultural land, mostly planted in alfalfa and with orange groves. Google the area today! What I recall was you could put the car window down in the evening, even in warm days in Phoenix, and the air was sweet and fresh with the smell of those alfalfa fields. In 2015 times had changed. The old highway 40 rolled out east, but then you had to drive south a few miles to the base via a two-lane rough asphalted road. There was no freeway (highway 60 or 202 or south 202) as today.

In 1968 and for years later the east valley, and then most of the valley was covered with a thin white layer of smog. This was the smoke from the copper smelters out east by Miami and Globe. The environmentalists fought it for years and finally won. The crap disappeared from the air and all we were left with was dust and Phoenix vehicular smog.

10. THE "OTHER LANGUAGE" - SPANISH AND ON THE JOB TRAINING AT ASU

Although I was hired, surely enough, to help develop the Portuguese Program, I was also to help out and complement the big push in the recently created Ph.D. program in Spanish Language and Literature.

There were several M.A. degrees: French, German and such, and many languages taught: Russian, Asian, Classics, but Spanish was the "dinner ticket" for the department. Why? Where were we? The Spanish Southwest and just two or three hours from the Mexican Border. Yours truly was a small cog in a bigger machine, but the role in Spanish would reveal much of university life and goings on across American Academia in the mid late 1960s. We were still feeling the effects of Sputnik, the Space Race and competing in the academic world.

Where to start? An underlying current, perhaps not much discussed in those terms, was that ASU was frankly "on the make." This young but rapidly growing metropolitan university had already butted heads with "Big Brother," the U of A in Tucson. A rivalry that continues today was just beginning. That is another long story perhaps, already told in part, i.e. Tempe "Normal" versus the University of Arizona in Tucson, the state land grant school - ASU's evolution to Arizona State College and then the state-wide campaign to be called "university" and the brutal and nasty battle that ensued. Credit should be given to the students themselves who spearheaded the movement for "equality" and the not small role played by the upcoming football program and coaches Dan Devine and Frank Kush or the nationally recognized track and field and baseball programs. But it was a state-wide campaign by students to get out the vote and win the day. Incidental to the battle was that the only law school in Arizona was at the U of A, and hence, most of the legislators in downtown Phoenix were graduates from there. But common sense and really the times prevailed.

So, the Ph.D. in Spanish was a bit of a correlating moment; the DFL and many other departments at ASU were on the rise. One must also not disregard the fact the President of ASU in 1968 was a Mormon and wanted to put his religion and people as well as Mesa and Tempe on the State Map.

A. SPA 101 ELEMENTARY SPANISH

As with Portuguese I volunteered first semester (and year) at ASU to teach SPA 101. This was unheard of for a young professor with Ph.D. in hand; most wanted to teach their specialty right off the bat. My program at Saint Louis University, Spanish and Latin American Studies, was a NDEA sponsored program with the purpose of providing teachers in critical languages and areas of the earth. I had a fellowship and not an assistantship, so there was no teacher training, nor did I ever teach a class (other than a very short stint helping in a language lab). The job was to study, to do research and to graduate. Thus, I came to ASU with absolutely zero teaching experience so there was no better way to get it than teach these basic courses, something I welcomed and as I said volunteered for. Somewhere I may say, from the very beginning I felt comfortable in the classroom and believe I had the "natural" instincts of the good language teacher; this turned out to be correct.

The SPA 101-night course turned out great; I got the experience but made lasting friendships as a bachelor at ASU. Two or three Engineering professors who wanted to spend time fishing in Guaymas, Mexico, and the like were signed up. We hit it off as colleagues, professors, and although none of them had a penchant for languages (as to be expected and was really the norm; my colleagues can't do math and engineering), their enthusiasm and friendship opened many doors for me at ASU. One person was Charlie O'Bannon a professor of civil Engineering from Albuquerque NM and a couple of his friends. Charlie really took me under his wing, invited me home to meet wife Nancy and the three small children whom I got along with famously. But there was more.

One of the engineering graduate students was at the tail end of a professional baseball career and was pitching part-time and going to class part time for the Phoenix Giants Triple A team. So, we attended a couple of games, talked to him as he warmed up in the bull pen and so it went. My life-long enthusiasm for baseball was whetted by this Triple A fun.

More importantly, Charlie, a white kid from a rough part of Albuquerque and a former Golden Gloves Boxer, had this over-the-top enthusiasm for Spanish bull fighting and the "macho" toreadors. When he learned that no less that El Cordobés the major "toreador" of that age in Spain would be doing a series of "corridas" along the Mexican border he immediately bought tickets and invited me along. It made for an event that was historic, never to be repeated. Charlie, I, and others attended the "corrida" in Nogales, Mexico, and saw an astounding feat: El Cordobés killed his allotted three bulls, was awarded no less than six ears, and did something else. He performed several "pases" on his knees with back to the bull. It was either a case of unparalleled heroism, an over-the-top desire to "shine," or stupidity. The man had a reputation among the "traditional" aficionados of the bull fight of being fool hardy and a show-off. Whatever the case, his story is one of the most interesting in the entire saga of the "corrida" in Spain. I touted the book "Or I'll Dress You in Mourning," his biography, for years at ASU. Thank you,Charlie.

There would be a meeting in Albuquerque later after Charlie had back surgery (related I believe to cancer) and would thereafter be confined to a wheelchair. But we shared many moments. Unfortunately, we eventually drew apart. So, we saw less of each other, but I have great photos of the kids and even later when wife Keah and I would see them when Charlie was on sabbatical at Oklahoma State U.

The night class of 101 turned out well and I learned the ropes. Gradually over the next few years, slowly and in the progression, I would do 102, 201, 202 and then the composition-conversation courses of third year. The latter was truly my baptism of fire at ASU and merits a telling.

B. SPA 313.

I drew SPA 313, Spanish Composition early in those days. The class was about 25 in enrollment, all Hispanics! Thus, all really were native speakers of Spanish and spoke at normal, high speed. My job was to assign compositions and grade them. I spent every night during the week and most weekends that semester buried in compositions with a Spanish-English Dictionary to my side and more importantly the Spaulding Spanish Reference Grammar, the best of its kind. This is when I really began to learn academic Spanish! Matters were not helped by the clique of good buddies from Nogales, Arizona, and Mexico who intentionally would pull pranks; always talk far faster than the professor could understand. But bottom line, they had to hand in the compositions and "face the music." I mention one person, rather famous in Arizona and California, one José Ronstadt. José, incidentally, not related to Linda Ronstadt the great Hispanic singer from Tucson, was also extremely intelligent and knew "good" Spanish. He married well, marrying into the ownership of one of the two major Spanish TV networks in the U.S. at the time. As a result, he did well. A lasting memory (it might have been "Univisión" or the US Western version of it, the name I cannot recall) was when he hosted the classic series and presentation of Fernando Rey and "Don Quixote de la Mancha." I give myself some credit for not bailing out during the months in that course but add one note from later years. Eventually the senior, native speakers of Spanish in the DFL would say that Curran, although not a native and with not-quite native proficiency (but still excellent) would be THE role model for Anglos who wished to study Spanish or Portuguese and make a career of it. I'll take that. I did not use the words "baptism of fire" lightly!

C. SURVEY OF SPANISH LITERATURE, SPA 321, SPA 322

As the years passed, I soon received the opportunity to teach the survey courses which I came to love and excel in. But a related note I remember, and which should be somewhere in all these notes was: the "system" of Spanish undergraduate and graduate courses and teachers at ASU. The old "naïve" gringo made another appearance (I've told in another book where my graduate advisor at Saint Louis University, Father Rosario Mazza, S.J., would tell stories of the students: "Curran is such a goodie-goodie he will be helping an old lady cross the street and she'll stab him in the back with her umbrella.")

So it was that Curran the young, inexperienced assistant professor went around to each of the senior Spanish professors asking their advice as to possibilities of teaching upper division Spanish Literature. Now, for those of you outside of academia, NO professor once he gets his hand on a favorite and "plum" course will ever give it up (except under duress like atomic attack or perhaps a heart attack). So, anything promising or fun like the courses on Golden Age Dramatists or Poets, or "Don Quixote" or the like was not in the works. It turned out that perhaps the 18th century Spanish Essay (easily the most difficult, the most boring and least desired course by students) MIGHT be available. At that point, I made one of the best and yes most practical decisions of my academic life: be content to teach the upper division but not graduate Surveys of Spanish Literature, which I loved, and continue the love affair with Portuguese language and Brazil. (Civilization courses, my cup of tea on the upper division undergraduate level would come later). So, I never taught Spanish graduate courses in the entire 43 years at ASU, but did do one upper division course, being "allowed" by a kindly Ángel Sánchez to teach "The Quixote" one time. I was able to publish and publish extensively in Brazil and that became the "ticket" to academic success and more importantly happiness!

One final thought, certainly after I had the highly sought after tenure, the tables were turned: when requested in the final years to fill a spot on an M.A. or Ph.D. committee for Spanish graduate students (and read the perquisite literary theory along with it), I said: "I'm not allowed to teach Spanish Graduate Courses (they all said you had to publish in the area to teach them, but this rule was never sustained, always there were exceptions), I really don't feel qualified to serve on your committee." There were a couple of exceptions over the years, and I did end up serving on several committees with students who had a minor in Luso-Brazilian, but by and large this was the rule. I was probably the most content, happy faculty member in the section.

Did this affect "prestige" and the like? Perhaps, they can all now consult my web page today and see if it all checks out.

After that digression, let's go back to the surveys of Spanish Literature. I must at least write a paragraph or two about them.

SPA 321

The course was from medieval times up to the end of the Golden Age. I got to teach and talk about the "Poema del Cid," Jorge Manrique, the great poets like Garcilaso de la Vega or Luis de Góngora, the dramatists like Lope de Vega and Calderón de la Barca, the "Lazarillo de Tormes" and finally Cervantes and excerpts from the "Quixote." Invaluable for all this were the many file folders of notes from graduate courses at Saint Louis University where I had a first-class preparation (see my book "Coming of Age with the Jesuits"). I was a "jack of all trades, master of none" at this, but did the job well, introducing and hitting the highlights of the Masters.

SPA 322

This course was less of a favorite, perhaps because my graduate school specialty was Golden Age, but still had some wonderful moments: the 19th century romantic poets and especially the playwrights whose plays were often adapted and converted to opera by the Italians, including the Don Juan theme, and "La Fuerza del Sino," and then fine twentieth century poets like Antonio Machado, García Lorca and a few others.

D. SPA 472 AND LATER 473

These were the rubrics for the upper division civilization courses in Spanish Language in the DFL. As with the literature courses, they were already "taken" when I arrived but a series of good fortune plus senior faculty being "busy" with other things enabled me to eventually teach them on a regular basis. Again, it merits some telling.

SPA 472

This course officially titled "Spanish American Civilization" was the catch all course for all Spanish America. It was based, at a minimum, on the "jack of all trades, master of none" type approach. Roberto Acevedo, an amazing Hispanic linguist with an M.A. from Berkeley taught the course. Roberto had one real claim to fame: he had an amazing memory and penchant for popular sayings, "adagios' and the like, all he once said learned from the prodigious memory of his mother while growing up (a like phenomenon was the prodigious memory and creativity along the same line of pithy sayings and phrases by W.C. Fields, something he also attributed to his mother growing up in Philadelphia). It turns out Roberto basically was tired of teaching the course and had no problem sharing it with me, and it turned out I "inherited" it with no complaints at all on his part. As far as I know no one else "coveted" the course.

It turned out to be my "cup of tea" based in part on the Ph.D. minor of "Latin American Studies" at Saint Louis University plus a natural penchant to do such a course. I had lively interests, aside from Literature from the major, in Economics, Politics, History, Geography, Religion, Music, Folklore and such and was prone to "inhale" anything about Latin America. Oh, that was the final note: because of my minor in Luso-Brazilian studies and the research specialty on Brazil, I incorporated that into the SPA course, keeping it all in Spanish Language I daresay. Perhaps of most importance, this is what truly broadened my horizons, interest and research and travel over the next thirty years. It would bring interest in a research trip to Colombia and the quest for the "Spanish Colonial Heritage" in 1975, directing the Guatemala Summer School in 1976 and 1977, and subsequent fundamental research on Pre-Columbian civilizations in Mexico and Guatemala for many years. The latter led to curiosity and study of Mexico, the Revolution, and the cultural roles of Frida Kahlo and Diego Rivera, long before this became a sort of "fad" in U.S. circles. There is no doubt it broadened the scope of both teaching and research.

E. POR 472 LUSO – BRAZILIAN CIVILIZATION

In later years, I did the same type of thing for POR 472 Luso-Brazilian Civilization, even more my "cup of tea." This was a piece of cake that allowed me to teach of the grandeur of Portugal's "Age of Discovery," the "Lusiads" of Camões, highlights of Portugal and then the main course: Brazilian history, literature, folklore and the like. There were many talented students, many who had never gone to Brazil, and I think I lit a fire under them. But also present were the ubiquitous Mormon RMs back from two years living in Brazil and who seemed to close their collective eyes when we really got into anything serious about history or literature. Not all of them, but most of them. They raved about how much they loved Brazil and were excellent linguists, but their world vision did not really include thoughtful consideration of some of our topics. Do I protest too much? Yes, in a sense because a few really did get "into" the material, and those I wish to remember best.

And finally, I can't recall exactly the circumstances, but the opportunity came to do SPA 473 Civilization of Spain. In this latter endeavor my expertise was all "book learning" with no genuine experience in-country. This did not stop me from applying a broad knowledge of Spanish history and literature, and a smattering of the same in art and architecture to giving a good, solid course. The culmination of all this would be finally in 1989 when Keah, Katie and I accompanied Professor Michael Flys, his wife Felisa and daughter Tamara on the ASU Summer School in Spain and finally in an intense eight weeks, saw most of what I had been teaching before and since. My recent book "Travel, Teaching and Research in Portugal and Spain" of 2013 (Trafford Publishing, Amazon. com) incorporates all I used to do in the course.

So that concludes an introduction and overview of what I taught at ASU for some 43 years. I'm sure the memory will be jogged for more as we go along. I wrote of Alan Sandomir, and there are a half - dozen exceptional students who became lasting friends; I'll plug them in as topics permit. I mean Connie Broughton, Terri Drew, Roberto Froelich, Larry Johnson, and Jim Emery. An added memory was of that "stacked" Latina who made an appointment one day, came to the office and in effect said, "I'll do anything for an A." She did not have to, nor did she.

11. MORE MISCELLANEA ON THE TEACHING YEARS AT ARIZONA STATE UNIVERSITY

A. THE EARLY DFL PICNICS AT SOUTH MOUNTAIN PARK AND PAPAGO PARK – SOCIAL LIFE IN THE EARLY DAYS AT ASU

The DFL Picnics 1, 1968

Check out a young John Knowlton, Sandy Couch, an unidentified youg lady, maybe Anita Knowlton, and George Carver. Great fun, great camaraderie.

The DFL Picnics 2, 1968

Here is a favorite Spanish graduate student from Alamosa State in Colorado, Keah my wife, a young Mark tossing the frisbee, Carmelo Virgillo, and Gary Tipton with the latest small fry in his family. Sites varied, from South Mountain to east Phoenix and Papago Park in the Buttes. "Those were the days."

B. BIKING TO ASU

Mark Biking to ASU

After that first bachelor year and perhaps when we bought our first house on Palmcroft Drive in Tempe about three miles from campus, Keah and I both purchased "genuine" Raleigh bicycles from the two brothers' bike shop in the tiny shopping plaza on the corner of Rural and Orange near ASU. This was in about 1973 and marked the beginning of at least 20 to 25 years of bike riding to work. Each fine bicycle cost $75. Frank Farmer and I once did a mileage calculation and I am positive that over all those years I rode more than 25,000 miles, or to put it another way, around the planet once! The three-mile one way trip from Palmcroft would be doubled in 1986 when we moved to Cottonwood St. in Dobson Ranch.

The route is fuzzy now, but I think it was out the door west on Palmcroft, carefully crossing McClintock at the Circle K, then a long ride west on Broadmore, and eventually over to College Avenue, up College across Broadway, then Apache and up the main mall to the LL building on the north end of campus. I would take the bike into the lobby, up the elevator, down the hallway to LL 442 my large office. There was plenty of room to stow it out of the way.

Clothing, cleanliness, showers and the like were a delicate issue, but it turned out with a good shower the previous night, plenty of deodorant and "drying off" in the office, helped greatly by a small table fan on high speed, it was all workable. I never used "biker's" attire other than the helmet, and clothing really changed during the season. More than any other factor it was the wind that was the chief concern, but except for fronts, I was fortunate: a prevailing east breeze in the a.m. and west breeze or light wind in the p.m. to blow me home. It's funny how all these trivial things go to make memories. I recall always trying to get the bike up to top gear particularly in the p.m. and needed a good tail wind to do it. And I kept an on-going record of how long it took to get home. Trouble is now I can't recall, but on Cottonwood I think I made it a time or two in just over thirty minutes. Then there were those terrible days with fronts and the wind was against me. That meant gearing down to second or God forbid first gear just to get home. I know either way it was a very sweaty affair, drying off and a shower at home in the p.m.

In spite of "Arizona" weather, it was very cold in the a.m. ride in the winter, I think leaving home about 7:00 or 7:15 a.m. I would do the "layers" routine, but always with a knit Bike hat under my helmet and covering the entire head and ears, and a neck scarf. Generally, a chamois shirt, windproof as they were, would do to stay warm. But by McClintock and the Freeway or a little beyond, the bike hat was rolled back above the ears and perhaps discarded by Rural, the neck scarf off and the chamois shirt unbuttoned.

In the early days, all my stuff was stowed in the old fashioned, traditional bike basket attached to the handlebars. In part II from Dobson Ranch, a longer ride, more stuff was needed. I purchased saddle bags which hung on either side of the back wheel. As I would "un layer," the stuff would be stowed in the saddle bags.

I was never afraid to ride on the city streets but was probably the most conservative rider on the streets. Part I was all on the back streets except crossing McClintock and Rural, and most times I got off the bike and walked it across. Actually, the most dangerous part in Part I was probably in that bike lane on College Avenue, safe enough as long as the single file cars and drivers were actually paying attention. You pretty much did have to be aware, constantly watching the rear in the bike mirror.

Part II was another matter, more complex and dangerous. In SW Mesa at Dobson Ranch, I would take Cottonwood to Baseline and get on the **SIDEWALK**, riding in that tiny "walk" space over the 101 Freeway. You had to get off the bike and walk it across due to the configuration of the bike-walk space. Then I stayed on the sidewalk (I would **NEVER** personally ride in the street on Baseline although many did) past River and then cut into the neighborhood zigzagging all the way to McClintock and on the sidewalk to the 60 Freeway. I stopped, looked at cars and probably rode the bike across the freeway bridge, that is, until the last days when I was a bit wiser, older, and walked it across. Then back on the sidewalk to maybe Hermosa, walk the bike across busy McClintock (if you waited there was a gap between freeway lights), and once again zigzagging to Rural, walk across that busy street and then a straight shot to College Avenue.

Mark, the Broken Wrist, Biking

Were there close calls? Not too many, but two or three more than I like to think about. I often told Keah that I was on "automatic" especially in the a.m., and often would arrive at school without much memory of the ride! There was one accident on the way to Cottonwood. I had turned the corner and was on the sidewalk east on Baseline toward the 101 when suddenly there was an elderly woman in the way. I slammed on the brakes, flew over the top of the bicycle, and landed flush on the concrete sidewalk. Result: one broken wrist, bruises and a bruised ego. If not for the bike helmet it might have been curtains. People at work used to kid me about the old woman and the bike, but such it was.

There is one overriding, pardon the pun, fact about all this: I am positive that it kept me in wonderful physical shape all those years and probably "banked" some for beyond. I know I sweated. (Katie and Keah tell me today my calisthenics and walking with barely breaking a sweat "do not cut it." Perhaps, but I'm not getting back on the bike.) One time, years into retirement, friend Ken Blood and I followed my route up to ASU one fine day. Perhaps because he is truly type A with a light bike or whatever, I was huffing and puffing, and we only did it that one time.

I was almost always alone on the rides and preferred it that way. You could think, remember the events of the day or just relax. I got to the point I would ride the backstreets with "no hands ma" and do some "windmill" arm exercises. I did ride a time or two near the park in Tempe before Rural with no less than Ned Wulk famous basketball coach for years at ASU; in this case he had been fired as basketball coach but either because of tenure or an agreement was teaching tennis or physical education classes before easing on into retirement. But the conversation was interesting.

There was a time when the ride home was with Tim Wong who at that time lived on Cottonwood in Tempe (before he bailed out for Ohio State). Enjoyable. One day Pier Baldini tried to ride along but had a defect in the bike and was huffing and puffing to keep up. That lasted one day only.

I just remembered: I passed much of the time singing old songs to myself or whistling the same; these were conjured up by street names which happened to coincide with the ditties.

C. TAKING THE BUS TO ASU

In the final years before retirement and during that nine-year part-time gig, I no longer rode the bike. It all started by chance one day when Quino Martinez told me how easy it was to get the bus on Scottsdale Road and no longer have to worry about driving and parking. So, I decided I would try this. It turned out to be not so easy with some funny moments.

To get to ASU by bus was not easy from Dobson Ranch. There really were three phases.

At first, there was no service until McClintock and Baseline. There you could pick up the Tempe Trolley (one of my students drove it). So instead of walking on Baseline the mile plus to McClintock I recall driving no less than our one ton dually truck to the SE corner of McClintock, parking it, and picking up the trolley. Its service was erratic, so a lot of waiting took place.

Later, there was improvement picking up old bus n. 72 up on Baseline and Don Carlos (It was just a ten-minute walk from the house) taking Baseline to Rural, north on Rural and then left on University Avenue, right on College and a nice cup of coffee at the Drugstore.

That got complicated when the city split the route: now it was two buses, the first n. 77 to the corner of Rural and then n. 72 north and eventually to College Avenue. The schedules did not mesh, so we would have to run like crazy to make the connection and perhaps miss it. And ditto for the return trip home. So, it could be at best a 40-minute affair but as long as an hour and one half. I got good exercise; when either missing or waiting for the connection east on Baseline in the p.m. I would check the time and walk a mile or more until the next bus would come, often in that sweltering Arizona heat.

I don't believe that any colleagues at all from my department at ASU did this. You see the "other side" of life: the clear majority of riders are minority, many are students, many on baseline headed to the GED degree program on McClintock and Baseline (a pretty motley crew, girls with purple hair, low cut blouses, many minority couples with baby and baby pack, young "hood" type guys with tattoos. And all were "wired" on the bus while I read my book or reviewed for classes.)

There was one "unforgettable" Reader's Digest style character: a black fellow probably in his late 20s, weighing close to 300 pounds, and of great disposition. He could scarcely get up the steps to the bus. We struck up a conversation once or twice, me trying to relate a bit by talking of old rock music. This kid knew them all! He would sing in a high falsetto on the bus all the old favorite Aretha Franklin Songs. It was the closest to on-bus entertainment I had experienced since the old Mexico City days in 1962! I know he got a part-time job as janitor at ASU later on but have not seen him for years.

And in the part-time years I would always run into Helene Ossipov (French, DLL, ASU) escorting young daughter Madelyn to Mount Carmel Grade School. Rick Boyle is her husband of Irish music fame. Madelyn was very much into the Irish Cultural Center and Irish Step Dancing (these were "River Dance" days). She at this writing attends the Catholic University of Portland and has spent summers in Ireland.

Otherwise, it was ho hum, hurry up and wait. But I could not get motivated for the bike.

A much later footnote - after the "final" retirement in 2011, after part-time teaching and losing my little token office in the basement of L and L, I still thought I needed a space to be at ASU. The answer seemed to be the Humanities Computer Lab on the third floor of L and L where I could work on writing projects. No actual new research was going on now. But it entailed another bike adventure, much more burdensome and not a long-lasting endeavor: I now had to park my bicycle OUTSIDE, thus necessitating a good lock, taking the saddle bags off each time (thieves were about and you would lose everything for sure) and perhaps packing a lunch. It was all a major pain in the butt and did not last long. I found I could work at home without all that. I am rather sure it was now that I began the healthy walks on the lakes in Dobson Ranch, an activity that continues today!

D. TAKING THE SACK LUNCH TO ASU

The sack lunch started at age six in first grade at Garfield Grade School in Abilene, Kansas, continued for eight years up to Junior High, a hiatus of four years with the high school cafeteria, then off and on again at St. Louis U. buying a sandwich in a local deli. I thought I was done. Then came ASU.

The sack lunch routine probably started when I married Keah in December 1969. It would continue regularly until 2011. Keah perhaps would have made the lunch some in early days, but for the most part I would make it nightly in the preparation for the next day at ASU. But she got the supplies. It was always a rather plain, but tasty sandwich of ham or roast beef and cheese, or often left-over barbecued chicken or the like, potato chips, carrots, an apple, and either three cookies or small miniature candy bars. The drink was the "ice" water from the fountain down the hallway and a cup of coffee later. Keah believes, and I do too, that this modest and healthy lunch for forty years probably goes a long way, along with the bike ride, of keeping me trim until retirement.

The exception was the Pizza with the Portuguese classes on Friday and when that phase of ASU passed, and it did, the onetime per weekly lunch with Frank Farmer or Tim Wong at Mama's or the Chuck Box or the like. In part-time later years we got a pitcher of beer to wash it down.

E. ACADEMIC PRESTIGE: UH OH. ASU.

Throughout the entire career there was the question of academic prestige: Ivy League or big-time west coast schools and me trying to compete for summer research grants with them using an ASU rubric. I am sure I lost out a few times. The best place to see the successful proposals is probably in the official "Curriculum Vitae" which lists accomplishments based on papers at academic conferences and then publications, but the "refusals" and such are only in my memory. Recently, an academic article by an Ivy League "big-timer" made headlines: he wrote an article on his failures in getting grants, notwithstanding the pedigree of his university. It took humility but as he said was of great value and encouragement to anyone in the academic game.

12. MORE LIFE IN THE DFL

I have written of the classes. This is all "the other" including a lot of miscellanea.

A. UP AND DOWN THE HALLWAY

My office was LL 442 near the north end of the building, the end that faces University Street. At the other end were the main office, the copy room with the refrigerator for the sack lunch, and most important the rest room. I would like to have a dollar for every time I made that trip. And many times, I made it whistling in the hallway (there were two of us whistlers, myself, and Doug Simmons of French and Language Lab fame). Did this irritate others? Perhaps. But I could do a pretty good version of "The High and the Mighty" and the main strains of Gershwin's "Rhapsody in Blue." Ed Friedman, the Jewish colleague in Spanish once commented positively on the latter while we both stared straight ahead doing our duty.

This was also the hallway that I rolled the bicycle down twice a day for umpteen years. And the hallway where I occasionally spilled coffee back when we used to get it in the copy room. But unlike some others I always cleaned it up!

What I remember most was what I would term a true "collegiality." You saw everyone from that Tower of Babel, and from my perspective all spoke, smiled, and perhaps a short conversation ensued. That is how I remember so many of the names on the "faculty" list to come.

And there were the bulletin boards, the requisite posters, class schedules, but mine was one of the most colorful with scenes of Mexico, Guatemala and especially Brazil. You could entertain yourself for a few minutes seeing the minutiae. Students would stop by.

B. COPIES FOR DAILY WORK SHEETS, REVIEW SHEETS, EXAMS AND THE SECRETARIES

For many years, such were typed by me on "ditto sheets" and run off on the messy ditto machine. The ink was blue and faded over the years. They then moved to a black and white ink machine, just a trifle better. It was only the final perhaps 15 years when we all got an account on the Xerox machine. I recall giving a typed copy of exams to the secretaries and would get my 20 or 30 copies just a few days later.

There was the one secretary, a great and great looking Jewish lady who was always with that Jewish humor, speech, and attitude. She may have been my favorite; this was during the Flys regime.

There was Donna Kaye Wollam always friendly but always with the latest news.

There was Eleanor a real DLL workhorse; we tangled a time or two and you had to know when you were on her turf!

There was Cindy the graduate secretary, and we were good friends although I had little to nothing to do with the graduate program. But she said most of the time was full of the travails dealing with the graduate professors.

C. DEPARTMENTAL MEETINGS

This was probably what I disliked most of the entire job and career. Particularly before the tenure decision there was no question as to missing a meeting. And after tenure I still considered it part of the job, so I attended. I had another mantra: do your minimum 40 hours ON campus. So I got to the office most days at 8 a.m. and certainly did not leave until about 4 p.m. Many colleagues especially the Spaniards were seldom seen, arranging schedules of perhaps two days a week and that even at night. Today I understand there is widespread change of my old guidelines. Working at home may be fine, but "show me the beef," i.e. the publications resulting from all that spare time at home.

There were section meetings for Spanish; Portuguese was handled with a short conversation in Quino Martínez's office. The former were of interminable length, and nothing ever seemed to be resolved.

There were the general departmental meetings, also of interminable length and really very little was resolved. When I was assistant chair to Peter Horwath for maybe two years it was my duty to write up the minutes and distribute them. (In exchange for very few duties I think I got a reduced load from 3 to 2 courses per semester and by that time I appreciated it.)

Mainly the meeting was determined by who was chairing it, his/her style, and manner. Some leaders could not close their mouths, others were a bit better. The absolute worst in regard to time dragging on was one of the Chairs of the Spanish Section. How I dreaded knowing what was coming up that particular 3 p.m.

It was the Spanish section that always provided the most fireworks. Paul Luenow once walked out of a section meeting with David Foster perorating over something: "Bullshit, David," and off he went.

D. THE ANNUAL RESEARCH CONFERENCE AND THE READING OF THE ACADEMIC PAPERS

This was "cast in stone" in the DLL of those days. You were, at minimum, expected to attend one "worthy" academic conference per year, read an academic paper which if good fortune was with you would be published in a "respected" academic journal. And of course, a few academic articles would one day perhaps be converted into a book.

I chose the meetings whenever possible due to their location, to see new parts of the country. The first was in Provo at BYU in the spring of 1970. Keah and I drove the blue Malibu that huge distance, were rewarded by snowcapped mountains on the central range, a handsome BYU, and a decent hotel room (ASU still paid for one night's lodging and per diem then.) But the main memories were trying to find the proper state liquor store to buy a six pack of beer, the smoke - filled bathrooms between talks (the only place all the smokers could ease their pain), and the final dinner at Sundance Resort back in the hills, deep snow along the way, and the "treat" of the Mormons allowing us to have coffee after dinner (but no booze).

Later meetings were a diverse lot, most linked to my interest in Latin American Studies (the SW Council of Latin American Studies; the Pacific Coast Council of Latin American Studies, the Rocky Mountain Council of Latin American Studies) but with a few special ones thrown in: The American Folklore Society in Philadelphia in 1976, the UCLA Seminar on Latin American Popular Culture in 1973, others I would have to look up, but the most important, an invitation to Brown University in Providence in 1994 and the company of the true New England "Portuguese" Academics but with great reception for my talk on politics and "cordel" and Sergio Miceli of the University of São Paulo press loving it and telling me to send it asap. Turned out to be the best accepted book of all in Brazil!

So, I spend time at USC, UCLA, a couple of the state universities in California, an occasional regional meeting in Arizona, and then the international stuff in Brazil (treated in my travel books). The worst memory was a Latin American Studies Meeting in Las Vegas (UNLV) with no less than Jon Tolman of U. of New Mexico and head of **BRASA** (the national Brazilian studies association), the chair of our session, and no one, I mean zero persons attended. We read our papers to each other. Keah and I did visit friend Mimi Lawyer and spend 10 $ on the slots on the Strip. A similar thing happened at the University of São Paulo in Brazil in 2002, another low moment in paper reading academia. In that case, not even all the people designated to give papers showed up. The session was scheduled late afternoon and intended for graduate students to reveal their research efforts. Fortunately, other goals of the trip were accomplished including the forwarding in the process of editing "História do Brasil em Cordel." On the other hand, there were the phenomenal experiences in 1973, 1981, 1990, and 2001 in Brazil (described in another book.) See my web site for the research side of things.

So, what to say? It was the "culture," the process of those years. If you wanted tenure and promotion you participated. What is most important in my mind is that I had the extreme good fortune of having a research area and topics which were extremely interesting and easy to convey to other professors and students (contrary to the opinion of one professor already mentioned). The proof is the 25 articles in journals and now twenty-five books published over the years. Perhaps I'll try to summarize at least the business of applying for tenure (and associate professor) and full professor if I have the energy.

The acquisition of tenure and promotion to Associate Professor revolved around a good teaching and committee record, a handful of articles but the tie breaker was the 1973 book in Pernambuco "A Literatura de Cordel" featuring the poetry, the poets and Ariano Suassuna. I think five years went by with a similar record, the chair then Dr. Michael Flys. I would have to check the Curriculum Vitae for details, but I think by 1981 the book on Brazil's most famous novelist Jorge Amado and "Cordel" had come out and there were promises for the Cuica de Santo Amaro book and the Rodolfo Coelho Cavalcante research was in place, so I applied and made it – Full Professor. In the later years after much persistence and travail they all came: books on Rodolfo Coelho Cavalcante in 1987, Cuíca de Santo Amaro in 1990, The Madrid Anthology in 1991, the **EDUSP** book ("História do Brasil em Cordel") in 1998 and a Hedra Publishing Company Anthology on Cuíca de Santo Amaro in 2000. During the final years before 2002 and the "first" retirement, I was hard at work, year - round, on what at first was "Portrait of Brazil – the Universe of the 'Literatura de Cordel'," and then "Retrato do Brasil." The latter would not come out until 2010, and then I began the Trafford Series, now some 30 books. I don't golf and you can't fish all the time, so writing and music it became and still is. More later on all this in the later years. There was significant volunteer work teaching Spanish or giving culture/travel talks at night at the local Bayfield Library in Colorado and music at church.

E. THE FULBRIGHT COMMISSION

A related topic was my good fortune and extremely hard work for the national Fulbright Commission. I was asked to read and judge applications twice, the first time in Washington, D.C. and the second in San Francisco. Keah was able to join me after the workdays for a wonderful time in those two places.

As a former Fulbrighter I took it all very seriously. I would have anyway. Memories are dim, but at least the first time they sent the applications ahead of time. It involved hours and hours of reading, note-taking, and a lot of tough thinking and ranking the applications. In Washington they put us in a hotel near Dupont Circle for three days. I ate meals from a deli across the street and worked day and night on the committee. During the day we would talk and argue the cases; at night there were more to read, and ranking. One memory is that the Ivy League and big-name school people did not give me or ASU much credence. But former debate work and a whole lot of homework enabled me to hold my own. I recall each night was later, the first perhaps midnight, the second two or three a.m. and the last maybe three or four a.m.

I was exhausted and "liberated" when Keah came to town and as a veteran of D.C., her degree from George Washington University, she really showed me the town: the subway system, the big train station up to New York, the Dubliner downtown, Dupont Circle, Georgetown, but mainly the capitol (you could still just walk into the balcony of the senate and house) and the terrific Washington Mall – the Smithsonians, Air and Space, the Gardens, and the National Gallery. We connected with Bob Burnett of Brazil and my own Fulbright days and had a wonderful dinner in Virginia. And there was also the Philips Gallery. Keah knew all the art galleries. It was wonderful and I was proud to be an American.

The second meeting was in San Francisco. Ditto the work; Keah came in the last day, and we "did" the town. Lodging was in a very modest hotel off Union Square, more like a B and B. So, we walked the city, art galleries (I am sure we walked by G. T. and Caterina Walsh's Japanese Art Store). A favorite was to go to the lobbies of all the famous hotels, have a coffee or a drink and take the elevator to the top. I recall the inverted hotel on the wharf of Mel Brooks' "High Anxiety" movie, the Top of the Mark for drinks, and the revolving taller one east of it. We did the cable cars and went to the Buena Vista down on the water for Irish Coffees and breakfast. What else? There were two or three later trips to the city, so I may be jumping ahead. But what a wonderful experience with Keah at my side.

The Fulbright work was also very important in building the Curriculum Vitae and perhaps the later promotion. I think I have never worked so hard in my life and in such an intense atmosphere as those few days.

PART II

COLLEAGUES AND MEMORIES

A

INTRODUCTION

    I would like to write of colleagues, some acquaintances only, some very good friends, who traipsed up and down the halls of the 4th floor of the LL building for almost one-half century. I suspect even before I start that I may not have as much to say about all this as I perhaps think now.

B

The Faculty: the "Seniors" and the "Juniors"

When I arrived in 1968, ASU was "on the make" and to a certain extent the DLL was also. There was a recent Ph.D. established in Spanish, many M.As. and other "minor languages" building programs. Hierarchy was based then on tenure, time at the U. and not necessarily research. That would start now and become a part of academic life. The "old boys" headed the committees and thus held the power, but all to varying degrees. Here they are.

C

THE DFL CHAIR WAS DR. HERBERT VAN SCOY

He was retired Navy, a gentleman and a scholar, a fair administrator who always treated me well.

D

THE "OLD LINE" FACULTY

The "Old Line" – those already at ASU when I came - Senior Professors in Spanish were Robert Bininger, Quino Martínez, María Escudero and Roberto Acevedo. John Knowlton was hired in the "old" regime and Ricardo Landeira from Spain as well. And Paul Luenow. Although coming "late" in 1964, David Foster was the moving force.

Bob Bininger was along the line of Dr. Van Scoy, the old school, an Anglo who loved Spanish. He was kindly and encouraging, later as well when he was an associate dean in the Liberal Arts College. His specialty I think was Golden Age.

Quino Martínez; I already talked of him regarding Portuguese.

María Escudero. Her degree was from Berkeley. She rode to school on an old bicycle, but in an old - style "granny" dress, quite a sight to see. She was linked to relatives in San Diego. Once again, she was always friendly and no hassles.

Roberto Acevedo, already mentioned regarding Latin American Civilization. Roberto was from El Paso, B.A. degree from U of A and still the best example I ever met with a natural "folk" knowledge of Spanish sayings, along with prodigious memory for such. He had an M.A. from Berkeley.

John, Anita Knowlton, and Mark in Colorado

John Knowlton could be a chapter here; a few notes are in order now. We became quite good friends; he was perhaps the best friend over the years in the Spanish Section. Already told were his days in Cincinnati. He got his degree from Oregon (and was a distance runner like me in high school). His first teaching job was difficult in a high school in a wild and (literally) wooly Pendleton, Oregon. He came to ASU's DLL and was the department poet. A truly sensitive person at that, John taught the 20th century Spanish literature, especially poetry. We swapped many stories of times overseas for research, the good and the bad, along with many lonely times. I think he spent time on a Fulbright in Venezuela originally, but Spain was his area. I know he wrote some poetry and contemplated it all at the Alhambra. He told of one occasion in Madrid when he was with perhaps Dámaso Alonso who informed him that on one occasion in the chair he was sitting and in the room were no less than Miguel de Unamuno and other major twentieth century poets, maybe including García Lorca. A high point in John's career. We shared all these things at the baseball games. John and Anita visited us once in Colorado; I read a eulogy for him at the funeral a few years ago.

Ricardo Landeira in my experience was the quintessential "Spaniard" on the floor. By that I mean I seldom saw him. I never had much contact with him until one fine day Keah and I along with colleagues in the Spanish Section received an invitation to his home for "tapas" and "paella." But his daughters come into play; Carmen the eldest and her younger sister were nice to me. It was Carmen's dissertation on "Cien Años de Soledad" that linked me to her because this was the first dissertation committee I was asked to serve on, in that first year of 1968. To her I owe my reading of "Cien Años."

Paul Luenow. Paul was also Ph.D. from Oregon, an old timer in the section. He, the Knowltons and I don't know who else made regular overnight trips to Nogales, Mexico on the weekends and thoroughly enjoyed the then safe and fun Mexican experience. That always included drinks and dinner at "La Caverna," where they claimed that no less than Geronimo had been imprisoned. The mariachis did not mention it. Paul did a lot of conversation and composition courses. His most memorable moment: the "Bull shit, David!" departure from a Spanish section meeting. Paul was always kind to me; he was the pipe smoker in the department.

David Foster. I don't know where to place David. He came in 1964 and in effect brought huge changes to the Spanish program. I think his Ph.D. was from Washington, but he first taught at the U. of Missouri where he met wife Virginia. He was I believe a genius (but interesting enough his father was a car mechanic and David knows his way around cars). One could write pages; he was the quintessential scholar of literary criticism and over the years and decades never failed to keep up with new waves of theory. Some said he was so far above the students' heads that it created a problem, but I have it that smart students loved him. His C.V. sported one hundred monographs and books over every conceivable style and period, and dozens of articles in learned journals. He was called and invited to the best of the conferences and presses. He did serve as Chair on one occasion.

David should have been at Yale, Harvard, etc. but asthma brought him to the Southwest; he was indeed a very big fish in a very small pond. He mellowed in recent years (have not we all?).

IN GERMAN THERE WAS INGEBORG CARLSON AND PETER HORWATH AND "FRA" TUTA SCHUBACH.

Ingeborg was indeed qualified, a Ph.D. in German from perhaps Heidelberg! She was an old timer in the DLL, and I doubt she published much, but was highly qualified. She served on many a Personnel committee, I with her in later years. In the hallways of the DLL, she always said "Hello young man." She threw parties and we were invited upon occasion, the German wine and champagne flowing.

Peter Horwath came a bit later, perhaps even after my time. He was a former seminarian, a bit of a social person from Prescott College. But he was a scholar European style – receiving the ubiquitous awards the Germans gave U.S. citizen – scholars. He in later years was a staunch Papist and claimed acquaintanceship with no less than Cardinal Ratzinger (later Pope Benedict). A Catholic traditionalist, he would do extensive research on Jesuit Padre Kino in the Southwest. Peter also threw parties, many as his time in Chair, with Korbel Champagne and the like. He was a pleasure to work with in my two-year term as assistant chair.

IN FRENCH THERE WAS ED GROBE, OWEN WOLLEM, AND DOUG SIMMONS RUNNING THE LANGUAGE LABORATORY, AND MIRIAM ABDOW.

Ed Grobe was another old-timer who carried a lot of weight in the French section and on committees. He was a musician and did some composing as well. Our friendship was more an acquaintanceship.

Doug Simmons was one of the finer gentlemen in the department. His French came from I believe WW II or later service and was impeccable. Due to just an M.A. or perhaps by choice he was relegated to language courses which he taught with fervor and lofty standards. He ran the

Language Lab and had enthusiasm for my work and particularly the "culture days" and Brazilian Music. He had his own airplane and flew to Mexico and later often to Florida. A good person.

IN RUSSIAN THERE WAS SANDY COUCH

Sandy was and "old timer" who started the Russian program but was a real maverick. He wrote his own Russian language textbook with Xeroxed copies for years. He had an elderly Russian lady as assistant for years until Lee Croft came. Always friendly to me.

IN LATIN AND GREEK THERE WAS GEORGE CARVER

I've told of George in another context. He was not only one of our best friends at ASU and the family, but a real quality person in the Department.

CHINESE WAS BEGINNING: THERE WERE NO "OLD TIMERS"

ITALIAN WAS BEGINNING. CARMELO VIRGILLO WAS THE MAIN FORCE. I'VE ALREADY TOLD OF CARMELO.

E

The Middle Line Faculty, I included, those recently hired around 1968 and there to help build the DLL were:

In Spanish David Foster was kingpin; I was beginning but "on track," Teresa Valdivieso was hired in the early 1970s after doing her own Ph.D. at either the U of A or ASU, as was Justo Alarcón the Spaniard from Galicia but "Chicano Literature" specialist.

Jerry, Mimi Lawyer

Jerry Lawyer who became my best friend at ASU for years, ABD the first year from Tucson, was hired to work with the Teaching Assistants. It was Jerry who invited us to camp on their property at Vallecito Lake in Colorado, introduced us to trout fishing in Colorado. Our life in Colorado after purchasing our own lot in 1972 was initially due to them. Thank you, Jerry and Mimi!

Maureen Ahern came on board in the 1970s, a wonderful preparation from years living in Peru, as did Stephen Dworkin in Linguistics from Berkeley, Flo Barkin in Linguistics, and Edward Friedman the Cervantes Scholar who later left the ASU scene for better things at Vanderbilt.

Gail Gunterman, a former Peace Corps lady was hired to ramrod the TAs and mother them. Flo Barkin was hired in linguistics and to work with teachers; she later moved on to Northern Arizona University in Flagstaff.

Teresa, Jorge Valdivieso, Mark

Teresa Valdivieso. She was the quintessential Spanish Catholic lady. Her background was little spoken of, but she worked for the U.N. in Ecuador where she met husband Jorge, a fine gentleman who taught for years at the Thunderbird School of International Management in west Phoenix. Her degree was from the U of A. She was a stickler in academics – she taught the graduate bibliography course and truly put the students through their paces, old MLA style. She always appreciated my Catholicism and Jesuit training; thus, we were on good terms. Conversation might include talking about Mass, the church. Only at her funeral at the "Casa" in Scottsdale (the Franciscan redoubt) did we learn of her extended family of earlier years. The funeral was classic Peninsular Spanish in style.

In German, there was John Alexander from New Zealand and Wayne Senner. John was proficient in German, but Latin as well. He had a biting sense of humor and satiric conversation. Wayne Senner's claim to fame was a seminar on the works of Beethoven, a success I was told. He retired early to his motorcycle.

In French Debbie Losse came aboard, Helene Ossipov a bit later and Alexandra Gruzinska from Eastern Europe. And a fellow who was an expert on Pascal.

Debbie, John Losse

Debbie Losse was trained at perhaps North Carolina, was married to John a mathematics professor at Scottsdale Community College famous for much higher salaries than ASU (Carmen Landeira landed there and was the head of Spanish for a couple of decades.) Debbie from the beginning was active on college committees, and the French section. She went on to be Liberal Arts Associate Dean and was Chair of the DFL in her last years. She in the latter capacity was always very friendly to me, very fair and encouraging. She did indeed keep the tradition of the DLL retirement parties and hosted a wonderful one (one of the last) for me in 2002. We saw John and Debbie a couple of times on the acre in Colorado (they hiked the San Juans). They retired to Sedona. Her demeanor as I recall could have been Ivy League. Classy.

Alexandra Gruzinska was from Poland (I'm sorry, I may be mistaken; it might be Romania), a serious teacher, and I think in 2015 was toward the end of her long career at ASU. (She will enter the scene in 2016 organizing the retirement "coffees" in the old University Club on campus, a big success.)

Mark, Lee Croft, Old Main

In Russian Lee Croft came aboard, ambitious, a former Golden Gloves Boxer from Cut Bank, Montana. He would become important in the section. Lee was always on the lookout for flaws in the pay system and unjust salaries. I joined him in one campaign about 1990 when I was ready to bail out of ASU for lack of raises, or significant raises (I never got to the point of sending out an application.) On a leave at Wichita State, he became knowledgeable of student marijuana and drug use in the work place, and together with wife Leslie started a drug testing business; it became highly successful, and Lee branched out with interests in Hawaii. Also, a rebel, he researched both literary and non-literary topics in Russia with some success in self-publishing after retirement.

Italian was soon bolstered with great days ahead by Pier Baldini, and as well as the Sicilian former racehorse jockey, Guiseppe from Wisconsin, and Chiara the TA.

Pier Baldini, ASU

Pier is a story in himself. Married young in Italy, time in South Africa, UCLA, Indiana and finally at ASU. Pier was a "par excellence" program builder. He almost single – handedly brought the Italian Program to national prominence, no less than by a very successful summer school program in Florence, his hometown. Pier had aristocratic connections in Florence, enjoyed the niceties of Italian life, threw great parties as Chair, and handled the "system," Italian style, to great success. My favorite memory: Pier told of the visit of Luciano Pavarotti to perform at Indiana University and socializing at Pier's house later. Pavarotti came in, went directly to the refrigerator, opened it and said, "I'll fix supper."

CHINESE

The Mormon President of ASU wanted "his boys" in the department; this was a natural thing with the in-country language training of two years on the church mission. Thus, RM Tom Nielson became "senior" professor and RM Gary Tipton junior but important in running the program. The first non-Mormon Tim Wong was hired from Stanford, and things began to change to reflect the new times.

TOM NIELSON was across the hall. Always pleasant, friendly, but in his own world. In that Salt Lake world in later years, he was "called" to be the head of the Mormon mission in one of the Asian countries, an offer he could not refuse, so Tom, spouse and family abruptly left ASU and academia. I have no knowledge of what happened in ensuing years.

GARY TIPTON

Tom hired friend Gary Tipton of the same persuasion, and they had a rather successful Chinese Program. Gary and I had good talks about Mormonism.

TIM WONG. TIM WAS/IS A GREAT FRIEND ACROSS THE HALL AND FOR YEARS TO COME IN RETIREMENT.

Mark, Tim and Lib Wong, Mark's Retirement Party

When Tim Wong came aboard, he added a Stanford flavor and Tim's penchant, Asian at that, for "important" Ivy League, Stanford, and Berkeley connections for ASU. Tim is one of my best friends from ASU days and I'll write at length of him. But the Chinese program developed good chemistry with this unlikely bunch (along with Madame Tu) to have a good program up to about 2002 and my retirement.

Over lunch and beers before and after retirement I learned of Tim's fascinating story: growing up in Canton, Hong Kong, the move to Hawaii, his father in Rio de Janeiro, baseball in Hawaii, working at the pineapple plant, the Portuguese people in Hawaii, St. Louis High School, sports writer, debater and then moving on to St Mary's in Moraga, Peace Corps Days in Thailand, then Stanford, Professor Lieu, meeting Lib, a year in Japan and the arrival at ASU. Our friendship has lasted for at least 40 years!

JAPANESE:

There was Tony Chambers who moved on to the Little Ivy League and came again (under the aegis of Tim Wong) to ramrod Japanese. But it was Miko Foard, Laurel Rodd, and Etsko Ryman who came to run the section after Tony retired. Tim Wong's wife Elizabeth ("Lib") was hired as lecturer and became a stalwart section figure.

And there was Tim Wixted in both Japanese and Chinese and with an office next to mine; lunch was sometimes slices of bread and a jar of peanut butter. He was a prodigious bibliographer.

There gradually was a smattering of professors for new languages: Arabic, Hebrew, Korean, and those from Southeast Asia.

F

THE "LATE ARRIVALS"

Some were "relatives" brought because of "important spouses" in other departments, "friends" hired and the like. I never really was informed in detail or appreciated the way it was done; this was a "new age," a sign of things to come in the expanding university. I thought you applied, sent in a "Curriculum Vitae", were interviewed by a DLL section or sub-section committee and then perhaps were hired. This did not always work that way. I was basically out of the loop, so those involved would have to provide the exact details.

In Spanish Cynthia Thompson came from ASU West, a specialist from Argentina. Emil Volek from Czechoslovakia suddenly appeared on the scene. Carmen Urioste was in Spanish. Two or three other Spaniards arrived: Ángel Sanchez, Alberto Aceredo who eventually left for a more ambitious career in Washington, D.C., and Carmen another linguist and teachers' professor; she came a little after I retired. These latter three, possibly, were brought aboard the "traditional" way with interviews, etc. I end with a disclaimer: perhaps the traditional ways were followed, but I was just not on the committee. Oh well!

As mentioned, Cynthia Thompson was a specialist on Argentina from ASU West; she added to the program, always friendly to me.

Emil Volek. A specialist on Literary Criticism, Avant-garde poetry, Cuban poetry, he would go on to at times chair the Spanish Section (ay, the long meetings) and would eventually offer a contrast of opinions with David Foster. Friendly to me.

Alberto Aceredo. Always quite friendly, quite competent, he was a good addition to the Ph.D. program; I'm not sure of his specialty. He left I understand for a good bureaucratic job in Washington, D.C.

Ángel Sánchez, ASU

Ángel Sánchez was perhaps my favorite Spaniard of all time at ASU. He was honest, hard-working, spent his 40 hours on campus, taught well the Spanish Surveys and the "Quixote" (after Edward Friedman's departure to Vanderbilt). He inherited as it were the Spanish Summer School and ran it quite competently for years, albeit, inheriting the structure Michael Flys had set up. We swapped many stories about all that, but I was never interested in going back to the school. Foremost, I recall his generosity in offering me a chance to teach the Quixote course, something I had always dreamed of, "just one time before I retire." After massive preparation (perhaps too much) I taught the upper division course and with very mixed results – it turned out to not be too much fun! I gladly passed on George Carver's cap and gown to him upon retirement; I hope he did the same for someone else. He was a good friend of Miguel and Felisa Flys and I would see him at their parties. His Castilian Spanish was a joy!

Somewhere he would talk of the Spanish classes, Foster and Volek, and the graduate program, and some inside news about it all. He kept saying I retired at a good time! He now has passed into the ASU sunset as well. Oh, I recall he had a background in international business, the wheat export business out of Minneapolis (he came from the U. of Minnesota) and we got along very well, who knows, perhaps due to my Bachelor degree in Business Management, I think in my final years and perhaps the part-time years. He was always a friendly face to converse with in the DLL.

Clarice Deal, Mark, Retirement Party

Portuguese: Clarice Deal arrived to teach the lower division Portuguese courses; she turned out great and expanded the Portuguese department with her expertise in on-line teaching, this after I retired. A great success. We had many good conversations.

G

THE NEW CHAIRS

Along the way there were new chairs in Spanish, duly recruited and interviewed.

Doug Sheppard came in from the U. of Buffalo in New York and a bureaucratic job in the Dept. of Education in D.C. And he had some "avant-garde" ideas about teaching. He was truly an "education" guy. He was always friendly to me, treated me fairly. I can recall the annual party, tee-totaling in tone, but we shared a love of trout fishing and that did not hurt. Tim Wong and I attended his funeral out in East Mesa a year ago in 2015.

Dinner at the Currans, the Baldinis and the Flys Families

Michael Flys is a long study and I'll just hit the highlights. He was my boss man on the ASU summer school in Spain. With some ups and downs, it was still a wonderful educational experience. See my book on Portugal and Spain that I dedicated in part to him, Felisa and Tamara. He came from Bowling Green University. His area was anything Spanish, but in particular Golden Age and 20th century poetry (he was a student of Dámaso Alonso's). It was his background that was unique in the department, born in the Ukraine, a refugee from both Stalin and Hitler, an "epic" crossing of the Alps to escape (he lived on goats' milk from the shepherds) and somehow admitted into Franco's Spain. He became more Spanish than the Spaniards but with excellent Castilian, a fine teacher, a decent publisher, but really with a talent for administration and program building. He singlehandedly made ASU's wonderful program in Spain a success, but he always invited and encouraged other DLL faculty to participate, my case one of them). But most of all he cared for the students, provided an educational experience and plenty of opportunity to party as well.

I think he may have hesitated a bit early on my promotion to Full Professor, but eventually backed it with some additional publications on my part for "ammo." He did tangle with some faculty, particularly regarding the question of translation for promotion (I remember one really "hot" meeting). But his standards were high, and he was good for the DLL. There is probably more to tell; he returned to the Ukraine in final years, the language came back, and he had some projects when I think prostate cancer got him.

Finally, there were those "ghosts" of the past, people who came for a year or two and for one reason disappeared: the linguist in Spanish from Berkeley who soon moved on to Florida, the Italian who did well drilling in the summer, the unlikely intellectual lady in Italian and many more I forget. Thus ends the story of colleagues in the DFL.

H

The Final Days, Why I Retired, and the Part-Time Experience for No Less Than Nine Years

Mark Emptying the Office, 2002

When I retired the first time in 2002, I made up a long pro/con list of why to do it; I don't' know where that list is today, but it was funny. I did it all with some tongue in cheek with "Catch 22" and that nervous, unsure officer who before he made any decisions got a yellow pad, drew a line down the middle and wrote "feathers in my cap" and "black marks against me." What I recall is that there indeed was a plan: retire **to** something and not **from** something. The list would be funny today in 2016, but here is a little of what I remember.

I was ready, classes and especially grading papers had become a chore. The students seemed less interesting, and I did not have too many favorites. The Liberal Arts College, wanting to get rid of senior faculty and their salaries (how ironic, mine was peanuts compared to most), offered a buyout of sorts, probably a pittance now. There was a $30,000 "accrued sick pay" coming; instead of buying a red sports car, I used that to pay the health insurance until Medicare at age 65. I regret the money being spent, but it was a good decision: it enabled me to retire three years early!

Somewhere in the narrative was the final day when the office was closed, I was on my bike home, rolling it outside the DFL building and overheard a coed on her smart phone in an amazing last conversation (details are vague now but it was sex, sex, sex and life at ASU). I recalled the amazing and funny conversation as I rode the bike down the mall for the last time. 1. The Retirement Party

Retirement, Mark's New Music System

Philip Leonard, the Retiree, Frank Farmer,
Gary Tipton and Judith Radke

Keah, Mark, the Retirement Party

A "new" life was promising in Colorado, all the usual stuff plus a chance to teach in the Ft. Lewis College Getaway Program (I did that for the summer of 2002, a course on the Mayas to all the retirees looking to spend a cool weather summer in Durango). But that was the year of the big La Plata County fire, maybe a coincidence, and Fr. Lewis dropped the program. "No Problem." I had projects and plans.

One plan became a return to playing guitar and singing in a bar. I "pounded the pavement and knocked on the doors" of prospective places in Durango and came up with Christina's Restaurant-Bar, first on north main and then across the river in West Durango. More on all that in another narrative, but it turned out well and I played once a month in the summer for about five years until "burnout" and a change in policy at the restaurant ended that.

A big event was when I took a deep breath, contacted Donna Lee Baxtrom at the Pine River Public Library near Vallecito Lake and began a series of classes in Spanish Language and then culture classes in English based on the old Civilization courses (and later Lindblad-National Geographic trips). Circa 2004. This lasted for quite a while.

I only mention in this narrative the tremendous, good fortune that followed the next fifteen years in retirement (along with the good already mentioned): The Library of Congress Conference in 2010, the Brazilian Cultural Center in New York in 2011 and 2013, and the three contracts for **LEX-NATIONAL GEO** the following years.

THE PART – TIME YEARS

The final note, and it will be short, was the time of part-time teaching at ASU from I think 2003 to 2011, doing just one upper division Spanish literature or civilization course, this to fill time in the Spring in Tempe and Mesa. I'll close this part of "ASU Years" with a summary and some thoughts on that.

The courses were at first fun; it allowed me to return to ASU two times a week in the a.m., have "office hours" in my cubbyhole office in the basement, but most important the two times a week lunch for food and beer with Tim Wong. We developed a fine friendship. And I got good exercise on the bike twice a week to ASU. This was also the time I "commuted" on the bus and met that cast of characters already described.

The students on the other hand were fulfilling a requirement; as always there were a few each time that were a pleasure. Many more were not. My memories are the difficulties dealing with the new technology just to show my civilization slides (the Mac and Microsoft platforms), but one final memory remained: the students all had laptops, ostensibly to take notes from the lectures, but most were on the internet.

I concluded: the time has come, my methods however good they are or were, are outmoded; times have changed. There is an on-going, ferocious debate in the Humanities and Academia: the old lecture-style teaching, which by the way I brought from Saint Louis University and practiced in upper division culture courses at ASU, was now considered "worthless by many" but not by some select others. Today I cannot recall one name of any student that remained with me from those part-time courses. So, was this all bad? Of course not, for the reasons above.

So, the "second" retirement came in 2011. In effect the next six years would be spent doing the memory, travel, and teaching books for Trafford, basically putting into print what I had taught for forty-three years, a very good decision.

And there is yet one "footnote" to this last experience at ASU: after stopping teaching in 2011, I decided I needed to get out of the house at Dobson Ranch a bit, so I bought a big bike pack, pedaled to the DFL building, parked the bike with its big lock outside, and went up to the Humanities Computing Center to do projects. It did not last long. I found I could work fine at home; get all the exercise I wanted on the Dobson Lake walks and still meet Tim for lunch a time or two a week. That basic routine continues to the present in 2016.

THE DFL RETIREMENT COFFEES

In 2016 a retired French professor, Alexandra Gruzinska, organized a coffee club for the DFL retirees. It continues to the present. Since it is part of the ASU memories, perhaps I'll add some comments and photos. Pessimistic at first about this, it has turned out well. Covid hit in 2020 and 2021; stay tuned for the future.

The DFL Retirement Coffees

And there was a recent visit to the Chuck Box, Mark and Tim's hangout and lunch spot for years. Aristeo Ponce the manager for 40 years, was at Burger King on south central in Phoenix, Chuck Box owner was there, met him and hired him to come to Tempe; the rest is history.

Mark and Tim, the Chuckbox

Addendum I

Campus Buildings
And Memories

Limited photos were taken recently, but most show ASU as it was in 1968. Because of limits in this book, only a few will appear in the text.

The first photo taken shows the north entrance to campus and the main north-south mall south of University Avenue.

The next is a scene of the busy North-South Main Mall between classes on a recent November a.m.

ASU in 1968 had an on-campus enrollment of 24,000 students, but the campus area was huge and allowed for much green space. There were three north-south malls and as many east-west. Although the buildings were spread evenly about, as I said, there was an abundance of all kinds of trees, many of them unique to the desert, but also many intentionally brought from around the globe. ASU was an official arboretum as well. Desert plants and an abundance of desert flowers were everywhere. And in those days, there were volunteers (retirees I think) who planted flowers year-round. Even without the "Ivy League" or UCLA, Berkeley or Stanford look, it was a truly pleasant place. One rode the bike up the entire north-south mall to my office.

SOME BUILDINGS OF NOTE

Historic to ASU but not particularly beautiful was the first building one saw entering campus on College Avenue from the south, coming on my bike ride to school over many years: old Goodwin Football Stadium. This was THE stadium during Dan Devine's great days and Frank Kush's earliest. In 1968 they had just completed construction of Sun Devil Stadium between the Buttes north of campus, as pretty, natural, and striking location as you could want in the Southwest (until they closed the north end in, you could see north to Camelback Mountain). I understand football players and other athletes were still housed in the depths of Goodwin, not a very pleasant accommodation I presume. It was an annual thing for many students to climb the west butte of the new Sun Devil Stadium, perhaps with a six pack of beer, and see about 50 per cent of the playing field from there. We did it a time or two just to experience the climb. Progress and an enlarged stadium wiped out the view later, but many students still made the hike with the six pack. And the ASU logo was up there, always painted red or blue by U of A scoundrels before the annual state rivalry game.

I'll just do a list of buildings I remember, not all memorable. The biggest criticism and valid at that is there never was any architectural unity at ASU over the years, thus my comment it was no match for the beauty and unity of the buildings at Harvard, Stanford, or UCLA, not to mention the Ivy Leagues or Brown University I would visit in 1994.

A new blue-glassed modern Business building on the North-South Mall was done on the right across the street north from Goodwin Stadium.

As one continued north on the mall, a great bike ride in the a.m. of a cool day, you came upon the old student union with administrative offices upstairs. It is not much changed today other than made larger over the years. My recent photo is from today and the main change is all the solar paneling.

To the east of the Student Union was the old, original physical education building with its small basketball gym where the Sun Devils played their games in 1968. There were intramural playing fields in the vicinity: tennis courts, basketball courts, perhaps soccer. An aside: one of the amazing sights for someone new to the Southwest was the flooding of the athletic fields and lawns, an unexpected sight in a desert! East of that athletic area they built eventually the "Computer Commons" which became one of the most important buildings on campus. In the early days, prior to laptops, I – Pads and smart phones, students jammed into the big space to use university computers. I even spent time there in learning sessions in early computer days.

East of that was the ASU Law School, a going concern when I arrived on campus in 1968. It was built under some duress with the usual battle with the U of A which opposed any law school outside of Tucson. A modern, round edifice, it was in the large auditorium style lecture hall where the first annual faculty meetings were held. It was there yours truly and the "new crop" of perhaps 25 faculty were introduced in September of 1968. Heady days.

A curious aside from those early days: one day my wife Keah and I decided to walk campus and one of the trees to the side of the law school was filled with Cedar Waxwings, a gorgeous sight not to repeated. It had to be a migration, but we were not "birders" in those days and could only surmise the reason for it all.

North of the Law School were some miscellaneous buildings I had little to do with. Central heating – air conditioning (the campus rests above a series of tunnels filled with support systems for the huge campus).

THE LIBRARY

The Library, ASU

Continuing north along the main mall was the library. The photo above shows it still as it was in 1968. I would spend hours filling out book order cards to bolster and build the Portuguese language and literature section.

The following photos show the new mall west of the library. A new underground entrance, much renovation, enlargement, and the computer age caused all this. I am told some students called the "obelisk" the "nipple of knowledge."

THE SOCIAL SCIENCE BUILDING AND THE LATIN AMERICAN CENTER – BACK TO THE EDIFICES ALONG THE NORTH – SOUTH MALL NORTH OF THE LIBRARY

Entrance to the Social Science Building, ASU

North of the Library on the Main Mall was "closer to home." This was the location of the Social Science Building which housed our Latin American Center. There were times when I had more to do with the Center than the Department of Languages and Literatures, my home base, reasons I'll deal with eventually.

There are some memories. The first director of the Latin American Center was Marvin Alisky. But he was good to me and gave credence to my research. Later I learned he was an "extreme" workout person, did the weights and liked to talk about it. He hailed from the University of Texas, a fine Latin American Program.

Second at the center was Lewis Tambs with a much longer more complicated story. I think he came from Creighton University in Omaha, one of the Jesuit Schools. His field was Latin American History and he had done some field research in Brazil. But he had also worked as an engineer in the petroleum fields of Venezuela up near Maracaibo. He once wanted to do a joint research paper on his research in the Amazon in Brazil. But I did do some translation for him, and in thanks to him, one of many great anecdotes of Brazil came out of it, i.e. The question of land ownership in the region, Tambs' interview with one such owner and a motorboat up a tributary of the Amazon for five days; "I own the land on both sides of the river." But the owner was not rich because there was no way to get products to market.

Lewis entered the story a second time: it was he who bought me a nice lunch off-campus, including a beer or two and succeeded in convincing me to be the on-site director of ASU's Guatemala Summer School in 1976.

Jerry Ladman was the last director; he inherited the center from Tambs (Lew became involved with politics with President Reagan. He had been Ambassador to Colombia, received threats to his life due to the U.S. policy on the drug war, so was then named Ambassador perhaps to Panama or El Salvador. He dealt with Iran Contra and the Shah of Iran business in Central America. Jerry Ladman was a very sensible down to earth scholar of economics and Latin American Business; his research area was in Bolivia. He helped me handle the second year in Guatemala and then bailed out along with several others from ASU to THE Ohio State University.

I recall working with Summer School Dean Dennis Kigin who provided terrific liaison for Guatemala, a fair and good man. Jerry Ladman by the way filled the Center with beautiful art and tourist stuff from Bolivia including one of those straw boats they use on Titicaca (and full sized!)

THE DEPARTMENT OF LANGUAGES AND LITERATURES BUILDING.

Mark Once Again Entering the DLL Building

It was north of the social science center and named appropriately for the times, "The Homer Durham Language Building," this for Mormon ASU President in the late 1950s and 1960s.

The first photo shows the main entrance from the north-south mall.

The second is from a recent walk-about on campus with friend and colleague Tim Wong in 2016.

The next picture from the walk - about is the north entrance to the DLL Building from University Avenue. This was the entrance/ exit we used for forty years to go to lunch at the Chuck Box on University Avenue and to Mama's for the first Brazil Club outings on Friday p.m.

Then comes a rather plain, uninteresting view from the east side of the DLL Building. One might ask "Why so important?" The reason is nostalgic; it was here I parked my bike for some of the nine years I taught part-time during retirement. I had been ousted from my old comfy large office on the 4ᵗʰ floor and moved to a retired faculty cubby hole in the basement. Most important was the loss of the space in the old office to park my bicycle. Thus, the racks in the picture; ASU was and still is notorious for bicycle theft, thus the long chain and padlock.

THE OLD HOPI CORN GOD FOUNTAIN AND OLD MAIN

The Hopi Fountain and Old Main

To the east of **DLL** is Old Main, the original "Normal School" of 1885 with its great park atmosphere. This was my favorite place on campus. It was and still is the only place on campus with some "traditional character," this due to the fact the two original buildings on campus from 1885 were located here.

The terrific Hopi Corn God fountain in front of Old Main (surprisingly Michael Crow kept it, a wise decision for the entrepreneur president of recent days and ASU's growth to 85,000 students; note in 2022: 80,000 on the main campuses in greater Phoenix; 60,000 on-line) and the new glass corporate structure of the ASU Foundation (for money raising) and the president's office on University Avenue to the North.

Other Buildings East: the University Archives Building, Palm Walk, the Mathematics Building and Engineering.

To the east of Old Main and the Hope Fountain was the old University Archives Building, the oldest on campus.

PALM LANE

Palm Lane, ASU

Between University Archives and the Math Building is the "Palm Walk" and the arched bridge over University Avenue, one of the old landmarks of old ASU. Student dorms are on the north side of university.

The old oval dorm was the first I saw when I arrived in 1968. The palms for me were the epitome of arriving to the desert southwest.

MARK AND THE MATH BUILDING OF 1968

Mark and First Office, the Math Building

Continuing on the east-west mall east of Palm Walk was the complex of buildings that included the "New" Math Building of 1968 and my unexpected office for three years at ASU. Its designer was Professor Nevin Savage whom I saw at am Emeriti luncheon in 2016.

And then there was the Engineering Building, "home" of one of my early, good friends Charlie O'Bannon, his wife Nancy. We met in my Spanish 101 night class in the Fall of 1968, Charlie and buddies wanting to learn a bit of Spanish so they could go to Guaymas and go fishing. They took me under their wing in those days and tried to arrange dates for me (not very successfully); the time of the "blond bombshell" and the bullfight in Nogales with El Cordobés.

Charlie, Nancy O'Bannon, Mark, 1968

In the empty space east of Engineering was parking with its original gravel lot, where I parked for 2-3 years for $5.00 per academic year; the entire area now is built up with new buildings, and the Light Rail on the NE part.

On the far south end is the Honors College with its prison-lookalike dorm windows. This is one of the worst architectural decisions at modern ASU. Ironic it is.

WEST OF THE MAIN MALL

Old Home Economics (today I think it is called family studies), the old administration building is in the back of the lawn a way down the mall. The "new" administration building in the late 1950s and my time in 1968 is one down the north-south mall.

The main administration building with the President's office was noted for its nice stairway and historic scenes of Arizona in nice murals; these were the "DIGS" of Grady Gammage and the Mormon president Homer Durham when I came in 1968, and then the great president from Vermont, Lattie Coor. I probably was in the president's office only once, a vague memory, I think an "introduction" of new faculty to the President.

All changed in 2002 my last year when Michael Crow came from Columbia U. in New York and totally upset the old way, "revitalized" the campus, and built the glass administration building north of University Drive. The Phoenix on campus enrollment in 2022 is 80,000 students! Plus, they are working to enlarge on-line learning! An aside: ASU athletics has never been the same. I was here in its "Golden Age" of late 60s, 70s, 80s, and 90s. (More later on this.)

THE NEWMAN CENTER AND CATHOLIC CHURCH

The Old Newman Center Church, ASU

Yet in the vicinity on University Drive was the old Catholic Newman Center where we would occasionally attend mass (along with the Leonards and others) and even participate ever so briefly in one or two Charismatic prayer meetings of the late 1970s. The Center belonged to the Diocese of Phoenix but was administrated for years by the Dominicans. They were progressive, liberal in tone for the most part. This became known and a few years ago the conservative Bishop of Phoenix replaced them with Diocesan priests. I am out of the loop, but it is a sign of the political times in Phoenix.

On College Street north of the Newman Center were bookstores, and my last hangout, the Campus Drugstore where I got a decent coffee to take to the office in the DLL and where you bought your ASU baseball hats! Next to the drug store was the bookstore where for years I ordered all my books and handout manuals. Bob Little was the owner, methinks another Mormon. We got along famously.

On old Mill Avenue in Tempe (the "famous" Mill Avenue according to party college rankings), and north along the Town Lake on land I am sure once belonged to ASU is now big-time business. Several of these projects went belly up in 2008 and 2009 but now are recovering.

On Apache / Mill in old Tempe in 1968 things were still rough, not the modern club/ restaurant area of today. When I was courting Keah, perhaps in the fall of 1968, I took her to the old pool hall on the west side of the street, a dingy place, and we played some pool. Our time was cut short by the arrival of a real motorcycle gang with all the accoutrements – we left casually but in a hurry. I think it was the Hell's Angels group from the sight of them, chains, tattoos, etc.

Returning to the north-south mall south of University Drive, other buildings on the west mall were more administration, the Graduate School, two big Education School Buildings, a new Lattie Coor Classroom building north, and the school of architecture which once again had windows with bars that looked like a prison. Farmer's Education Building (secondary education) was an occasional place for me when we as new faculty in Spanish in 1968 were obliged to evaluate student teachers in Secondary Education-Spanish in the Phoenix area. You drove your own car, in my case to downtown Phoenix Union High School to do the observation. It was the secondary education faculty who ramrodded this.

GAMMAGE AUDITORIUM

Gammage Auditorium, ASU

Finally, on this part of the tour of campus was the large sector directed to the Fine Arts. The crown jewel was Grady Gammage Auditorium, "The Birthday Cake," with astounding architecture. It was rumored that the plan came from Frank Lloyd Wright and was originally destined for one of the sheiks of the oil rich Middle East who turned it down and ASU happily inherited it.

Gammage would play a major role in entertainment for Mark, the bachelor, and then Mark and Keah. Now historic shows of Johnny Cash and Marty Robbins, and more importantly the classic guitar greats of the world then – The Lutenist Julian Bream, Andrés Segovia, the Romeros, Christopher Parkening, and flamenco guitarist Carlos Montoya were part of those good times. (In "The Guitars – the Music Odyssey" I write of John Denver in the basketball arena in Addendum II to come, the basketball arena jammed with his fans, circa 1970s, 1980s.)

The "little brother" of Gammage was the ASU Music Building which we frequented for M.A. and Ph.D. student recitals over the years. One professor, Caio Pagano from Brazil, was a "star" and later Regents' Professor of piano, his office was in this building.

The ASU Art Museum and Fine Arts Complex was nearby.

ADDENDUM II
THE ASU ATHLETIC COMPLEX

"A" Mountain, Today's Light Rail, the Edge of the Football Stadium

The Crown Jewel of ASU athletics was of course Sun Devil Football Stadium (it replaced the old Goodwin spoken of earlier). I don't know when they started it, but it was complete in the fall of 1968, and I attended a game or two with the blond T.A. from the language department. And a memorable one with colleague and great friend Jerry Lawyer and his wife Mimi. ASU played the Air Force Academy and we saw a Peregrine Falcon do its stuff at half time. Just a year or two later it was expanded in the form it kept for years until now in 2015 they are spending millions to remodel.

THE ASU FOOTBALL STADIUM

ASU Football Stadium, Sunset and Lights

THE BRONZE STATUE OF ALL – TIME FAVORITE COACH FRANK KUSH

Our Hero, Football Coach Frank Kush

This was the "House that Kush Built" and recalls the era of great ASU football. There are dozens of anecdotes, and one needs to see the "Hall of Fame" pictures in the basketball oval to see the dozens of nationally famed stars. Joe Spagnola, Danny White, John Jefferson etc. were among the greats. One anecdote, just like the battle to become ASU, was the other battle to gain national recognition for Kush's teams. No one wanted to play them because the outcome was certain, a loss in the bowl and a loss in prestige. We old timers remember that ASU practically begged for a place in the Peach Bowl in Atlanta, perhaps in 1970, was accepted, and annihilated I think North Carolina in a snowstorm! The problem was not solved; there were still no invitations the next year, so ASU and Phoenix began an institution: The Fiesta Bowl which ASU dominated for years.

Then Frank Kush rattled the helmet of an incalcitrant kicker and was fired for his disciplinary action (recall similar things happened to Woody Hayes of Ohio State and Bo Schembechler of Michigan State a bit later.) The athletic director who did the dirty deed happened to be the same one who built the new ASU basketball arena and then bailed out to take over San Diego State's program. Sour grapes? Hell, yes.

Somewhere I write of that early excursion with Peter Jackson up ASU Mountain to the west of the football stadium (six pack of beer in hand) to have a taste of the tradition of climbing the cactus and thorn filled path to get just a glimpse of an ASU game. They later expanded the stadium for sky suites and TV media, so the view was indeed blocked out, but students still make the climb. And of course, the big golden ASU "A" is at its top, painted red and blue annually by U of A Students and then repainted golden yellow by the fraternity crowd at ASU.

WELLS FARGO BASKETBALL ARENA

The Wells Fargo Basketball Arena

To the southeast was the 14,000 - seat basketball arena seldom to be filled, except possibly when the U of A came to town. And the Olympic swimming pools, dive boards and stands are south of that. I went to a game or two of basketball in the new area, one battling Ohio State, Ned Wulk still our coach. Interestingly enough I was with Tim Wong who later taught for a few years at THE place. The seats in Wells Fargo were crammed together, as for very small people, but the photo gallery of all the ASU greats was great and yet a memory today. Later I would attend ASU women's basketball with terrific seats behind the bench, my benefactor friend Ken Blood. It was there we saw an exhibition game and the great Diana Taurasi, one of the great athletes, man or woman, I have ever seen.

ASU TRACK AND FIELD AND THE STADIUM

Those photos also showed our great track and field teams (with several participants in the Olympics, a 300-foot javelin thrower, Mike Murro, and my attendance at the Sun Bowl Invitational for years). I just read of Henry Carr's death; he was an Olympic star on the team. In the same vicinity to the east of that there is a vast array of tennis courts south of the track and field oval. I used to attend the "Sun Devil Classic," ASU's lesser version of the Texas, Kansas, or Penn Relays. Oftentimes I would meet John Knowlton and we would enjoy the races and swap stories of our high school track and field days, John I think in the mile run, me in the 880 (see "The Farm" for all those stories, among them the 63 second quarter mile in practice while "goofing around," and the maybe 2:28 half mile in the cold rain at the State Track Meet in Hutchinson.)

ASU PACKARD BASEBALL STADIUM

Packard Stadium, Later Days, Mark

Then, most important, was Packard Stadium the home of ASU baseball and a plethora of stars that became even greater stars in Major League Baseball. At one time ASU was to be feared, always a participant and many time winner of the college world series in Omaha. Reggie Jackson and Barry Bonds for openers. And Mike Kelley who hit one over the center field wall one spring. Truthfully, there was a big wind out to center field; I attended this game with our visiting professors from Mexico.

I would attend games regularly over several years with ASU still great in baseball. There were many games with John Knowlton talking of Spanish, Spain, his growing up poor outside of Cincinnati but seeing the famous double no hitter of a Redleg's pitcher of those days, perhaps Johnny Van der Meer. Many times at Packard were with friend Steve Angel (New York City), catcher on CCNY's college team, who played baseball for the

Army in Viet Nam (and umpired). Steve and his wife Terri and Keah and I met at St. Timothy's Catholic Church on a couple's retreat in Prescott, attended Pope John Paul II's visit to Tempe and the mass and pope mobile in Sun Devil Stadium, and socialized since. They took care of our daughter Katie on one of our trips. Steve was a very successful broker during those days before retirement; he had tickets to many major sporting events in Phoenix. Due to his kindness, I saw San Francisco play the Cardinals in ASU's stadium with quarterback Steve Young, Michael Jordan in a game versus the Suns, and Randy Johnson defeat the Yankees in the 2001 World Series. Thank you, Steve.

Steve knew all the baseball parlance ("frozen rope") and baseball history, so we were a good match. I would take a clipboard, a yellow pad, and keep score most games (to keep interested).

And I attended many baseball games as well with Tim Wong, and we talked of the language department and baseball. Tim was high school sports reporter at St. Louis high in Honolulu; he recalled "listening" to major league baseball (received by wire or telegraph) and the announcer then "announcing" the game.

All of this gradually ended when ASU did less well and all of us losing a bit of interest.

Today it has all changed; they will tear down Packard Stadium (Tim and I saw Packard field with a parking lot on the diamond in 2016; I was in shock) and sell condos in its place to pay for the remodeling of the football stadium. North parking lots will hold tall condominiums; an inflatable football practice field is east of Rural as are all the softball and whatever venues. I think I can safely say it WAS one of the best overall athletic complexes in the nation, and surprisingly enough, if you include "minor" sports ASU is still highly ranked across the nation each year.

My memory fades for the moment. Enough already. But the reader does have an excellent overview of campus.

A recent "threat" in 2017 was an "offer" by the ailing Phoenix Coyotes Hockey Professional Team to build a spanking new area on the old ASU

Golf Course east of Rural (the course made famous by Phil Mickelson), the "carrot" being a smaller arena to the side to be the home of ASU's fledgling hockey team. Fortunately, and probably miraculously, some old timers spoke up and it was axed in the state legislature. A few years later they got their wish: they will share a spanking new hockey arena with the ASU team.

In these same years they have torn down Packard Stadium, moved baseball to the old Phoenix Muni Stadium across from Papago Park and the zoo. The latest, a small tidbit, was a short article in February 20, 2017, by a "Phoenix Republic" reporter lamenting the fact that ASU employees can't take that "sick day" and sneak over to Phoenix Muni Stadium for spring training with the Giants or A's. They now have to go to Scottsdale or the West Valley. Muni is now controlled and run by ASU, the unexciting home of the Sun Devils (due to the gigantic dimensions of the ball park that took away almost all the home run baseball of ASU – I'm waiting for them to at least bring in the fences). And ASU bought/leased old Papago Golf Course immediately north to become the "official course" of ASU (the old one on Rural according to the newspaper will end up as condominiums by Michael Crow to build the "remodeled" football stadium).

I took many more photos of the sports complex, but there are too many for this Trafford book. But one can go to the Sports Museum on campus or the basketball arena and see them. I will present a list of those taken from the Sports Museum, great memories of ASU Athletic History.

1. Frank Kush
2. Charlie Taylor, Curly Culp, Danny White
3. The "Catch" by John Jefferson
4. Track and Field Champions and Olympic Medalists – Mark Murro (I saw the wind-aided 300-foot javelin throw), Henry Carr, Ulis Williams, Mike Barrick, Ron Freeman, a world record in the mile relay
5. Sun Devil Baseball Stars, Album 1

6. Sun Devil Baseball Stars. Album 2
7. A night game at Packard Stadium
8. Early Baseball Stars, a photo, Roger Schmuck, Sal Bando, Winkles
9. Bobby Winkles
10. The Tradition: Eddie Bane, Mike Kelley, Bob Horner
11. Jim Brock
12. Reggie Jackson
13. Rick Monday

CONCLUSION OF "ASU DAYS"

For now, I've said what there is to be said. For the nitty-gritty story of duties at ASU, committees, but also the research, foreign travel and publications, see my website www.currancordelconnection.com, Books, Bio and Curriculum Vitae. If by chance, and that is a slim chance, any surviving colleagues see this, I hope it jogs the memory in a good way! And for others, friends, relatives, acquaintances in Arizona and perhaps retired professors at other places, it might be fun to compare notes and remember their own days in academia. Thank you.

September 2022

BOOK TWO

THE GUITARS
A MUSIC ODYSSEY

Mark J. Curran

TABLE OF CONTENTS

THE STELLA – STEEL STRING. ABILENE 1955

The Stella Guitar

THE KAY ELECTRIC – ABILENE - 1957

From the Spanish Club Banquet

The Kay Electric

THE $50 SEARS – ROEBUCK NYLON STRING CLASSIC

ABILENE - 1959

The Only Photo – A Student Party in St. Louis in 1964

The Sears – Roebuck Classic – Student Party in St. Louis

THE DIGIORGIO CLASSIC - RIO DE JANEIRO, 1966

The DiGiorgio Classic, Rio de Janeiro

THE MANUEL RODRÍGUEZ ELECTRIFIED CLASSIC, ESPAÑA 2002

The Manuel Rodríguez in its case

PROLOGUE

While doing the "coffee walk" early one morning on Deer Trail Lane in Colorado in the summer of 2022, perhaps June 13th or 14th, and as usual, wondering what my next writing project and Trafford Book would be, it came to me! Like so many times before, there was a flash of a topic and then some general ideas until I got home. Unfortunately, this time I did not write them down … until now.

The guitar and music have been such an important part of my life, from age 14 in Abilene, Kansas, until now at age 80 and counting in Arizona and Colorado. I've written of this in several books, accounts of the topic in autobiographies such as "The Farm" and "Coming in Age with the Jesuits.," But this "lampejada" or "flash of light" was different. Let's see if I can explain.

I want to write about a lifetime of music, of learning to play the guitar, the different kinds of music I played and still play, even maybe a "primer" on how to play some of it, and the different instruments I had at one time or another. And the pieces of music as tastes evolved and my exposure to different kinds of music took place. And of course, in part, singing went along with it. I've been blessed with an "ear" to know if I am "in tune," and can stay in tune and also know if the guitar is in tune. But also, as Mom would say, I was gifted with "a nice voice." A pleasant voice. Hmm. It's not a great voice, not operatic like brother Jim had, but more like brother Tom or sister Jo Anne's. I remember they were all in school choir especially in high school and all three sang in the church choir at St. Andrew's.

For some reason, choir, or organized groups were not for me; I was more of a loner, but that did not mean I did not like to sing. I think I was in the Abilene High School choir senior year but was not a stalwart member. I could sing the first melody line, but never did have an inkling for singing second voice or harmony. Nor did I have one of those outstanding "solo voices."

Singing would take place the last two years of high school when I teamed up with buddy Eddy Smith, both of use somehow managing to get out of afternoon study hall and go into the empty band room, tune up our electric guitars and small amps and play the "pop" tunes of the day. I'll get back to this.

Let's see how it goes. You got to start at the beginning.

1

THE MUSIC STORE
AND THE STELLA

The Stella Steel Stringed

It is 1955 and I am fourteen years old. The picture above is of the Stella I purchased with hard earned chore money from the farm for $15 dollars cash.

Before I try to recall that day, an explanation of sorts about me and music is in order. Mom thought I should be introduced to music and that happened in the second grade. I took piano lessons from my Godmother Mrs. Lexow who lived near St. Andrew's church on south Buckeye in Abilene. I think there might have been some "mom collusion" because good buddy Mike Kippenberger also got saddled into this. I think lessons might have gone on for a few months. I did do some practice, but our piano in the music room on the farm was out of tune and some the keys would just produce a "thud." But I hung in there because Mrs. Lexow gave us milk and cookies at each lesson. I was pretty good with the right hand, but never did get the left hand in sync. End of story.

The second "chapter" of music training was in grade school band with Mr. Worman (he had a thin, trimmed mustache, wore coat and tie, and seemed very serious). I played a rented silver clarinet, was in fact first chair maybe in 6th grade, but ran into a problem: Mr. Worman said my clarinet needed to be cleaned, and we honestly did not have extra money around, so I balked. I can't recall how it ended, but that was the last of me and band. Oh, I do remember some marching on the athletic field. I thought that might have been the most uninteresting time I ever had experienced.

Sorry: there must be aside about marching. I am a huge fan of Joseph Heller's "Catch 22" and heehawed many times when he told of Lieutenant Scheisskoph. The Lt. was in charge of the base marching contest each Saturday morning. His goal was to win the symbolic flag for the next week for his platoon. He was so obsessed with the marching that he neglected his beautiful, stacked wife who spent her time screwing the airmen in the platoon.

On the other hand, I protest too much. One of the great memories of growing up in the 1950s and 1960s was to watch the college football games on TV and see the sparkling marching bands at halftime. There was one band from one of the southern Black schools that really put on a performance and was unsurpassed.

And it was possible to get a scholarship for band to college back in those days if you were good and qualified; one of our high school girls got the "full ride" to Oklahoma University.

I did learn to read music while in grade school band, at least the rudiments, i.e. quarter, half and full notes, treble clef, 2/4 time, waltz time. Just the basics.

So, when I brought that Stella steel string home I was not starting from scratch. It has been a long, long, time but I must have had a basic guitar method book. I learned how to tune the instrument and was playing some basic melodies but using a pick or plectrum. The pick was heart shaped, and you held it between your thumb and forefinger on the right hand and struck or "picked' the string. The fingers on your left hand were on the fingerboard to "fret" the note. A tune had to be really basic, maybe a Burle Ives folksong like "Goobers Peas" or Dad's favorite, "Jimmy Crack Corn" or "Swanee." Funny, an old memory but they all are important:

There was a 30-minute program on TV on Sunday Nights, GE Theater, and I think Ronald Reagan hosted it. The sponsor was "20 Mule Team Borax." How about that? On the night in question Burle Ives was the star (there was a different guest star each week for the program). He was a hangman, traveling on a circuit in the old wild west. He was in town to hang someone but happened to play the guitar and sing to pass the time. Hmm. I'm sure he played "Goobers Peas." I had no idea then of how important he was in American Folk Music, in that age of Woodie Guthrie. I loved Burle Ives.

Ours was truly a musical family, Tom on the trumpet, Jo Anne on the violin, and big brother Jim with a fantastic baritone almost opera quality voice. I've already mentioned they all sang in church choir and musical shows from high school. An important part of life at home on the farm was when we gathered around the old RCA Victrola Record Player in the "middle room" upstairs.

We sang, ad nauseam, the old ditties from the 1920s or 1930s on those quarter inch thick records. There were lots of Irish songs like "I'll Take You Home Again Kathleen" or "Danny Boy," but also songs I might hear years later in a W.C. Fields Films. One in particular sticks in my mind called "My Little Bimbo Down on the Bamboo Wire" – "Daily, daily, you'd make a hit with Barnum Baily." But by far the most records were old tinny versions of John Philip Souza marches or old Irish.

It was brother Jim that I owe for the big change in music and my evolution with the guitar. I don't know if he intended it that way or if it was just a whim, but thank you, Jim! He was a traveling salesman for Ehrsam Manufacturing in Enterprise, Kansas. The company made passenger elevators for grain elevators or the like. Jim at one time or another was a purchasing agent for materials to make the products or an estimator for jobs. This took him often to Kansas City, Missouri, and on one of those trips he brought home a Classic Guitar Method Book by a Mr. Van der "Something" from South Africa. He gave it to me, and I took to it like a duck to water.

I want to describe all this in great detail, and hey, maybe even give a "primer" or lesson. The music, the tunes, or the songs I can't recall now, but I might possibly play one or two yet as warm up exercises. I'm sure they were just the basics. I tried to look up South African Music Primers for Classic Guitar, but no luck. It has only been 60 years.

The most important thing is that method book introduced me (or anybody) to the basics of playing classic guitar. Just for openers: you held the guitar cradled across your left thigh, the nut at the top of the neck about even with your left shoulder. You should have a footstool to put your left foot on, maybe four inches from the floor. I did not have one of those but think I just stacked several hard back books up and that did the trick. You were to "fret" the guitar, that is, curve your left hand around the neck and press on the places of the strings you wanted to play. There was a huge item which I only realized later: a major rule for classic guitar! The left thumb was placed on the back of the neck or at most just slightly on the side (this in total contrast to all kinds of country, rock, blues, and who knows who else of entertainers who use the thumb on top maybe fretting the sixth string).

So, I began to play very basic scales, introductory exercises and mainly plucking with thumb and first three fingers of the right hand, (pmi on the music). I might add that in those days we had 33 rpm records of the guitar music of Chet Atkins. He was a master, and I tried totally unsuccessfully to imitate his "finger picking" style. But note: he used thumb and the first, second and third fingers of the right hand, but all with circular picks a bit like having a ring on the end of each finger! Someone in the family, I don't know who, had picked up a 33-rpm record with Chet playing classic guitar (without the picks and again a master). My hero.

Then a major thing happened, still with the Stella. It did not stop or interrupt the classic interest but was kind of "parallel" to it. I think Mom, Dad and I were attending a local 4-H Club meeting out in the country near the farm. I guess they were there because I could not officially drive at night yet. The boring 4-H meeting at some point was interrupted by the time to sing those old corny Kansas songs. A young lady got up, a guitar strap around her neck and back, a basic six-steel-string non – electric guitar across her chest and sang "You Are My Sunshine." A light went on in my brain, or maybe a lightning flash! She was singing and accompanying her voice strumming on the guitar and playing chords, I now suspect the three basics for the key of C: C, F, and G7th. She held a pick in her right hand as she strummed across the strings and her left hand held down the respective strings on the correct fretting for the chords. I thought,

IS THAT ALL THERE IS TO IT?

Mark was now off on a new adventure, singing and playing, using the chords I would soon learn from a basic twenty-five cent guitar chord book. Don't get me wrong; this did not happen overnight! I soon learned some keys were a lot easier than others:

C C, F, G7th
A A, D, E7th
D D, G, A7th
E E, A, B7th
G G, C, D7th

The "bastards" and really unplayable for me were the others: Bb and F.

The whole world of minor key came into the story, but more limited. I played,

E minor: E minor, A minor, B7

A minor: A minor, D Minor, E7th

Keep in mind I was still playing solo as well so whatever those notes were on the page, regular, flats, sharps, I learned to fret them with the left hand and pluck them with the right. But this was when I discovered, duh, you can sing songs and accompany yourself on the guitar.

I would become fairly proficient at many of these basic exercises or pieces and then one big piece: a simplified "Malagueña."

2

THE 1950s, TEENAGE YEARS, EARLY
ROCK N' ROLL AND POP, 1958-1959

I'm not here to write a history of the evolution of music in those years, nor do I have the knowledge to do so. But I've got to talk some basics and rudiments to explain how things evolved for the guitar and me. There are, it seems, many "threads" to the story.

1. The arrival and dominance of the electric guitar and its role as the main instrument in all the music popular let's say in my high school years of 1955 to 1959. Whether it was country music (really little played or appreciated in in my crowd at Abilene Public High School), or the many strands of "pop," principal among them early Rock n' Roll, its artists, and mainly Elvis Presley. And the "white" pop of Ricky Nelson or "That"ll Be the Day" by Buddy Holly. I can only remember more if I were to see the old "Top 25" Pop song books we began to buy at the "dirty bookstore" on the corner of Buckeye and Third Street. The shop sold "standard" magazines and newspapers as well, and anyone could go in and buy. But the memory was that the scruffy owner's Mexican Chihuahua dogs were allowed to run free and poop on

the magazines displayed lying flat on the first shelf off the floor.

2. 1955. That was the year brother Jim brought home from the appliance store in Enterprise, Kansas, where he worked at the Ehrsam Manufacturing Company two items: a perhaps 21 inch black and white television set and more important a tall antenna you had to put up on the roof of the farmhouse to pick up any stations.

I had watched TV before, once on a blurry black and white set, me enthralled, at a restaurant Jim took Mom and me to on a day trip to Kansas City. More often was watching the tiny black and white TV set at friend Clarence Gellinger's place on Highway K-15 North of Abilene where his dad ran an auto repair shop. We would watch wrestling and Amos and Andy on perhaps a 12-inch screen. But 1955 was different.

TV changed our lives; not all at once, but in a relatively short period of time, maybe two or three years. From the days of the first black and white and we could only get three stations, only one fairly clearly, from Hutchinson, and two fuzzy, from Wichita and maybe Kansas City, to the rapid improvement of I guess transmitters when we could get clear views of CBS, ABC and NBC. A whole fun chapter I could write would be to recall all the shows we watched as a family (See "The Farm), and most important, really moral fare, funny, innocent and not a speck of what we would call "immoral" programs. The big moment, Jim once again responsible, was the arrival of a color TV set which really changed us – the Wide World of Disney the real winner.

But in 1955 on a Sunday night "must" watching was the Ed Sullivan Variety Show and I think the GE Theater. Once again, many pages could and have been written. For this narrative there is one item: 1955 and Elvis Presley's first appearance on the show. Elvis with long hair in a ducktail haircut, swiveled his hips to "Heartbreak Hotel," or "Don't Be Cruel." Teenage girls swooned and us guys were just as excited. Elvis would return to the show many times, but now his songs were high up on the "wish list" for Mark Curran and his buddy Eddy Smith at Abilene High School to learn and play.

3. I do not remember any details where the money came from, but I am sure it was earnings from the farm work in the summer for Dad, but probably by age 17 in 1958 I bought a Kay Electric Guitar and a small Sears amplifier. The Stella was still around, but we are now in a different era. Eddy had the same, an inexpensive electric and amplifier, and we both cajoled someone (no idea how) that our studies were up to date, so perhaps a better use of time would be for us to practice "music" in the vacant band room of the high school during the study hall hours in the p.m.

Below is a vintage photo of that Kay, albeit on a different occasion one year later: it had a shiny copper finish, much like the paint jobs on the custom cars of the times. And Eddy and I both played the electrics with a pick, a heart shaped piece of plastic held between thumb and forefinger of right hand.

The Kay Electric and Malagueña

I would need to have one of the "Top 25" or "Top 50" Songbooks from almost 65 years ago to tell you what we played. I do know that I was playing chords and singing, Eddy was doing the same but could do some "riffs" between verses and sing in harmony. We possibly reached a repertoire of maybe 25 songs.

The kicker, and it's funny, was this was a real melding of Curran the white, Irish American guy and his culture, and Eddy, the black All-American boy and his culture. We both liked early Rock n' Roll. I'm trying to just remember a few of the tunes:

Bill Haley and the Comets - "Rock Around the Clock"
Buddy Holley - "Peggy Sue"
The Everly Brothers: "All I have to do is dream." "Wake up Little Susie"
Ricky Nelson: "Poor Little Fool"
And Elvis:
"Heartbreak Hotel"
"Blue Suede Shoes"
"Don't be Cruel."
"Jailhouse Rock"

And Eddy knew all the black hits of Chuck Berry, Little Richard, Fats Domino and others. He and the Black kids in town had their own group and sessions where he said they would "wail."

"Lucille"
"Bebopalola"
"Young Blood" (I saw her standing on the corner, a yellow ribbon in her hair)
"Gonna Rock it up at the Ball Tonight."
"Blueberry Hill"

We knew the words to them all, and the standard chords, nothing fancy:

C/F/G7

E/A/ B7

A/D/ E7

G/C/D7

There was probably a lot more Eddy knew he wasn't telling me, but oh, did we have fun. I don't think the volume in the band room was that high, but surely you could hear it if you walked by in one of the hallways. It all culminated in our only "gig," playing one night after supper for the girls in the cafeteria of sister Jo Anne's class up at Marymount College in Salina, Kansas. We both had cowboy hats and jeans on (Why? I remember no country and western) and must have played for an hour. And it was a rip-roaring success.

Years later, there was an informal "reprise" of those songs, but probably now sprinkled with some country and western. I was working at the ice plant in the summers in Abilene after senior year in high school and first year in college; Eddy was at Ehrsham's in Entrprise. At night in those hot summers, we would go out to the bandshell in Eisenhower Park, sit on the benches or picnic tables and play and sing those songs. High school buddy and drummer, Bob Hensley would join us at times on the bongos. This was after drinking ten cent draft beer at Howie's Tavern on 3rd street in town. The police would cruise regularly just checking in on their normal route, and as long as we kept it down, there was no problem. I do think by then it was just acoustic guitars, me on my "new" Sears Roebuck $50 classic and Eddy on I don't know what.

There was one night when good buddy Mike Kippenberger and his cousin Jack (of much greater fame later in the FBI), both doing farm work that summer, came by and we sang some country songs. Hank Willliams to be sure. Titles? Lonesome Whippoorwill.

Just a related aside: Eddy and I were about the same level in sports, just average and not a bit above. I would have him out to the farm in the summer to play catch with our baseball. His mother told my mother years later, after his untimely death as a very young man, that he always treasured those moments, the first and only time he had ever been on a farm. There were no Black farmers in Abilene, the only historic area where they tried was to the northwest in Nicodemus. Eddy and I had good times.

3

BACK TO CLASSIC GUITAR AND "MALAGUEÑA" 1955 TO 1959

Around that same time, I was always working on the very basic classic guitar pieces and exercises on the Stella steel string. It all culminated in that scene already alluded to with the Kay Electric when senior year I played an ersatz "Malagueña" on the electric at the Spanish Language Banquet.

Just a quick aside (already written of many times, but on this exact occasion): it was the guest appearance at the Spanish Banquet of two IFYE – International Farm Youth Exchange – young 4-H'ers dressed in bombachas, gaucho belt and boots, that inspired me to continue the study of Spanish and perhaps minor in it at college, to come. It took about 50 years before I ever made it to a gaucho ranch in Uruguay and then on to Buenos Aires.

I do not have available today the exact exercises, but I was beginning to study many pieces. Today's list of 2022 follows, but just for reference. Many were not tackled until graduate school days, or practice at home in the many years in Tempe and Mesa while teaching at ASU or perhaps during retirement.

I. Quick Classic (memorized). This is the "fantasy concert" played almost daily in practice at home in Arizona or Colorado.

Exercise 1,2,3
Etude: Carcassi
Romance: España, 1930, anonymous
Allemande. Bach
Fugue. Bach
Prelúdio. Heitor Villa-Lobos
Estudo. Heitor Villa – Lobos
Mexican Piece
La Cumparsita
Le Tambourine
Für d'Elise. Beethoven
Green Sleeves
Malagueña
Flamenco: (sort of)
Huelva. Montoya
Zapateado. Montoya
La Zambra. Montoya

II. THE LIFE-LONG STUDY LIST, NOT MEMORIZED, AND STILL A WORK IN PROGRESS AFFECTED BY SOME ARTHRITIS.

1. Come with me my Giselle. Adam de la Halle. 1230-1287
2. Greensleeves
3. Six Lute Pieces of the Renaissance. Anonymous. 16th century
4. Pavana. Luís Milán. 1500-1561. España
5. Dance of the Washerwoman. Hans Newsidler. 16th century
6. Mistress Winter's Jump. John Dowland. 1562-1626
7. Españoleta. Caspar Sanz. 1670-1710
8. Minuet. Henry Purcell. 1659-1695.

9. Allemande. John Dowland. 1562 – 1626.
10. Brayssing. Study
11. Gavotte. Alessandro Scarlatti. 1660-1725
12. Minuet fácil. J.S. Bach. 1685-1750
13. Prelude for Lute. J.S. Bach
14. Allemande. J.S. Bach
15. Fugue. J.S. Bach
16. Minuet (difícil y lindo) J.S. Bach
17. Preludio o Capricho. Caspar Sanz. 1670-1710
18. Pavanas. Sanz
19. Prelude. Robert de Visée. 1686
20. Bourré Visée
21. Bourré II. Visée
22. Gavotte. Visée
23. Gavotte II. Visée
24. Für d'Elise. Ludwig Van Beethoven
25. Sonata quasi una fantasia. Beethoven
26. Romanza. Nicolau Paganini
27. Arpeggio Etude. D. Aguado
28. Estudio 1. Francisco Sor. 1778-1839
29. Estudio 2. Sor
30. Estudio 3. Sor
31. Estudio 4. Sor
32. Estudio 5. Sor
33. Estudio 6. Sor
34. Estudio 7. Sor
35. Estudio 8. Sor
36. Estudio 9. Sor
37. Estudio 17. Sor
38. Andantino in E Minor. Sor
39. Waltz in A. Fernando Carulli. 1770-1841
40. Waltz in E. Carulli

41. Allegretto. Carulli
42. Recuerdos de la Alhambra. F.Tárrega. 1852-1909. A challenge.
43. Leyenda. Isaac Albéniz. 1860-1909. A challenge.
44. Prelúdio n. 1. Heitor Villa-Lobos. Rio de Janeiro. 1940
45. Estudo n. 1. Heitor Villa-Lobos. Rio.
46. Romance para Guitarra. Anónima. España. Circa 1930
47. Bach Fugue in D. ***

4

THE NEXT CHAPTER – MUSIC AT ROCKHURST COLLEGE - 1959 TO 1963

When I moved into the dormitory (Xavier – Loyola Hall) at Rockhurst College in September 1959, there was not much luggage: some clothes, but not many, trip kit, my new Smith-Corona Electric Typewriter, and my Sears – Roebuck Nylon String Classic Guitar, the latter stored under the bed on my side of the small room to be shared with James Fitzgerald of Concordia, Kansas.

I have written much in other narratives of times at Rockhurst, but just as part of the total experience. I now want to write of the music itself. What I can remember:

a. Practice of Classic Guitar in My room or in the Basement of the Dorm
b. Playing the Kay Electric in the Continental All - Stars Dance Band
c. Playing Classical and Mexican Songs for the Latinos at Parties
d. Playing the Kay Guitar in the Blue Velvets "Rock" Band
e. Playing the Kay Electric in the Slim and Curly Show at the Rockhurst Variety Show
f. Playing Fifteen Minutes of Classic Guitar for the Variety Show

g. Post – Rockhurst Graduation: Summer of 1963 the 50-50 Club for 10 weeks.

An Aside: So many years have gone by, and memories are fuzzy. I am sure I bought the Sears – Roebuck via the store catalogue for $50, probably in the summer of 1959, probably with earnings from working for Dad on the farm or possibly from the Belle Springs Creamery Ice Plant in Abilene for Paul Huffman. Memories are hazy, but I know I played it all four years at Rockhurst. (In Guatemala, I played a borrowed guitar for the Matheu family; that and my Spanish might have caused Julio Matheu to make the job offer, see "Coming of Age with the Jesuits"), and all the years at Saint Louis University to come, from 1963 to 1968.

A. PRACTICE OF THE CLASSIC GUITAR IN THE DORM ROOM AND IN THE BASEMENT ON WEEKEND NIGHTS

Sorry, but once again the memories are just kind of general. I know I never practiced when roommate Jim was in the room, but there seemed to be a lot of time when he wasn't so I would get out the Sears guitar and I think work on the classical pieces. More of a memory were the many times I would come home to the dorm on a Friday or Saturday night, maybe after some beer drinking with buddies at Sammy's Tavern on the Kansas side, or maybe after an early movie, or even a dance in the Rock Room at school, not ready to go to bed.

There were small study rooms downstairs and they always seemed to be empty. I would take the guitar into one and play perhaps for up to an hour, and I'm sure it was the Classical. No singing. For the life of me, I don't know the exact pieces, but I'll bet they included the "warmup" exercises and pieces:

Three "exercicios"
Etude Carcassi
Le Tambourine

Romance

And probably the "Malagueña." I had a 33 RPM record of Spaniard Carlos Montoya playing "flamenco" music, and I could manage to work my way through 3 of his pieces, never as fast and probably leaving something out:

Huelva
Zapateado
La Zambra

And it must have been then that I was learning some Latin American solos, maybe "La Cumparsita" and maybe I did sing old favorites like "Cielito Lindo."

A lot more would come in the three years later at Saint Louis University when I think I acquire more classical music, and where I started to learn Brazilian Portuguese.

Now, was I "buzzed" on some of those nights? After Sammy's for sure.

B. PLAYING THE KAY ELECTRIC IN THE CONTINENTAL ALL -STARS DANCE BAND

The Continental All-Stars Band

I think this picture is far more impressive than the reality. It was probably 1959. The trumpet player, his name gone for the moment, was the instigator. He was from Chicago! And, incidentally, he was Jewish. That is an aside in itself: the first Jewish person I had ever met! He brought a lot of Jewish "swagger" and big city "swagger" with him, had very definite ideas about what he wanted to do, and largely did it. Charles, that was his name, was, well, intense. (Quoting another famous song, Irish it is, McNamara, after all, "I'M the leader of the band!") Me, I was just a "grunt" in the back row, probably there for the lack on any other guitar player in school. I know the band was modeled on the "real" dance bands of the 1930s, 1940s, or maybe 1950s, the Glen Miller Band the only one I can think of.

We played dance music, I guess, and there was no singing (bad luck; those early bands always had a great female singer). Alas, Rockhurst was not co-educational. We practiced in the p.m. in one of the empty classrooms in the science building (Sedgwick Hall?). I still had my small amplifier and the Kay Electric from high school days. I'll comment if I can on the band, and apologize ahead of time, as familiar as the faces are, names and details are gone today, almost 60 years later.

My friend then, and best friend from St. Louis, was the pianist, Bill Bockelman. Bill will enter my music story much more four years later when I will move on to Saint Louis University for graduate school. Bill played well, and in fact had a valuable tool of the trade – the "fake book" or three-inch-thick "encyclopedia" of old standard songs of the times, just with basic melody line and perhaps chord names. With one of these, if you were good, and Bill was, you could play just about any simplified version of those songs.

Charles did try to maintain what I guess was a "classic" dance band tradition (I knew zero, zilch, nada of any of this; it could have come from another planet). Between refrains and verses, etc. by the entire band, individual "solos" were in vogue. Bill could always handle a few of those. He could play some Dixieland, and even Scott Joplin.

The main soloist, however, think a bit of a small-time version of Gene Krupa, was the drummer. Our man was Phil Kezele, he of my first night roommate experience at Rockhurst freshman year. I tell about it in "Coming of Age with the Jesuits." We both talked of how we liked music and Phil kept me up most of that first night with radio music. Nothing was said, but he switched roommates the next day, a mutual decision. Entertaining American Irish boy Jim Fitzgerald of small-town Concordia Kansas close to home in Abilene turned out to be a good choice for me. Phil could indeed play those drums and had the classic personality of the showy drummer.

An aside, I can say it now. Phil is resting peacefully somewhere. I never did appreciate drums, in fact, thought they were often too loud and disrupted the music. But I was an ignorant farm boy. Later years would grow my appreciation of the timpani person in Music in the Mountains of

Durango Colorado. The All Stars would all stop, rest, and let Phil carry on for what seemed an eternity. I do believe that most, many, some people really liked his solos, the big band tradition. Somewhere, maybe the Ed Sullivan show on TV, I saw Gene Krupa perform and must say Phil did a good imitation.

The three sax players I recognize and remember them all, except names. Vince was one. God bless you and forgive my memory.

The trombone player, ditto. I remember he was from a small farm town in northern Missouri, had a terrific sense of humor and was an all-around good guy.

Bill Bockelman is in the back on the piano. Next to him is the guitarist on the Kay electric. When it came time to solo, I knew one tune: Honky Tonk. Period. I must say it was an education learning the chords for dance band accompaniment. 5ths, 7ths, major, minor, I'd have to see the chord manual. I remember then and know that I was never enthralled with the guitar's role as rhythm instrument in dance bands. It seemed like it was used mainly as a percussion instrument. Such big band guitarists seemed to be playing big body electrified Guilds, Martins, or the like. But this was a good experience; we probably played three or four "gigs," and maybe made $10 each. It all folded when Charles graduated.

C. PLAYING CLASSICAL GUITAR AND MEXICAN SONGS FOR THE LATINOS AT PARTIES AND THE INFAMOUS "SERENATA"

There were very few times when this happened, once I think at a picnic with the Rockhurst Latinos and the Notre Dame de Sion Latina girls. I knew so few songs in Spanish, and I am sure they were just tolerated. I recall one young boy, I think perhaps from El Salvador, who had a really fine voice and could sing the Italian "Al di la." But one moment suffices for all.

These heady days in the early 1960s were still the times of the traditional "serenata" in Spanish America. The young man wants to please his "novia," perhaps celebrate her birthday, or maybe even propose marriage. He hires a fine group of mariachis and all troop to the residence of the young señorita. She is plied with beautiful songs like "Las Mañanitas," the birthday song in Spanish. Tradition has it, if she likes the performance, she will throw her "novio" a red rose from her balcony. Much folklore.

Whose idea was this in perhaps 1962? I'm thinking Ernesto Townson of Guatemala or perhaps Eduardo Matheu, but it really happened. After getting oiled up at a local beer bar, perhaps Probasco's Dragon Inn on 55th and Troost, we piled into someone's car, drove to the iron gates of Notre Dame de Sion, that nuns' boarding school for all the very wealthy Latina ladies to learn French, perhaps English, and become nicely "finished." My buddies dated some of them, albeit in very traditional nunnery-protected fashion. Someone decided we should have a real Latino "serenata," once again, albeit "no mariachis, mon." Mark would play the guitar, and we would all sing "Las Mañanitas," "Cielito Lindo" or such.

We parked the car (or cars, who remembers), crawled over the iron fence surrounding the convent-school, ensconced ourselves below the window of what they surmised was the girls' dorm, and began the serenade. I have little or no memory of details, but perhaps a young lady or two applauded or said "Viva." But then the colegio's guard dogs tuned up, Dobermans to be sure, and soon police cars arrived, red and blue lights ablaze. I do not know if there were sirens, but the bottom line was something like this: "Muchachos, la fiesta se acabó, vayan a casa a dormir." No arrests (it would have been an International Incident, and we all retreated to Xavier and Loyola Halls.) A moment never forgotten by some folks.

There has to be a footnote. Only incidentally of music. I actually dated one of those cute girls, not really dated, but perhaps "chaperoned" to a dance or two. I think she even invited me to the prom at no less than the Muelbach Hotel in downtown Kansas City. Surely, we did not go in my rattletrap Dodge, but perhaps all in a rented limousine. One Patricia Raynal (perhaps correct or not) of Parral, Chihuahua, Mexico. A final memory: after summer vacation that year (it must have been my junior year) she returned from old Mexico with a diamond ring on third finger, right hand, that one could not dare look at in broad daylight for fear of blindness. I'm not sure today I would recognize her if I saw her (I mean the 1958 Patricia Raynal); today she is surely an "abuelita").

How many North American students of Spanish can recount such days and events? All I know is the Spanish did improve. My gringo friends in fact voted me "Outstanding Foreign Student" my senior year.

One of the social moments senior year related to the Latinos was the time I decided to stay in Kansas City for the Christmas holidays, probably cutting the umbilical cord from Xmas in Abilene. Eduardo Matheu told of the prospects of a good party at an apartment on the Paseo with some TWA stewardesses. The problem was there was a blizzard, deep snow, too much to drive. Somehow, we wangled a small sled, put my guitar on it, and headed down the hill from Rockhurst to the party. I guess I played the guitar a bit, but that was it. No stewardesses tho'.

D. PLAYING THE KAY ELECTRIC GUITAR IN THE "BLUE VELVETS" ROCK BAND

After that earlier foray into playing in bands, I mean the "Continental All - Stars" perhaps freshman or sophomore years, there was probably a six-month stent in another band. Details are fuzzy; it could not have lasted long, but for sure during spring "prom" season.

Probably through the auspices of Bill Bockelman once again, I heard of, was introduced to, and invited to join "The Blue Velvets." It was the times my friend, the beginning of Rock n' Roll and the national phenomenon of pop bands and music everywhere. But with a couple of curious points.

Our leader, a fine young man who really could play solo electric guitar, founded the bunch. He lived in the very wealthy area of perhaps Shawnee

Mission or Overland Park in Kansas City, Kansas, but was a student at Rockhurst. A curiosity, and just a hazy memory to be sure, was that the family fortune was due to the manufacturing company of condoms, "rubbers" in our parlance. The connection to Catholics, a Catholic education, and a Jesuit young men's college? There is none. But we talked about it.

I think Phil Kezele was the drummer once again, Bill on piano, me on rhythm guitar, and another member or two. The band's forte were the snazzy instrumentals led by our leader; one title suffices: Guitar Boogie Shuffle. I tried for years to learn it and never made it past second base. I was allowed that old standby solo of "Honky Tonk." I think we might have even sung a song or two. We played a local dance or two, I think at Catholic school mixers, but the culmination was, well, sort of big time! The classic "band from the big city coming out to the college town for the spring dance." Ha ha ha ha ha. We loaded up all the equipment and drove out to Manhattan, Kansas to Kansas State University to a spring fraternity party.

I remember little, business as usual with the songs. But the high point was we each earned the astronomical amount of $25 each. We drove blearily into the "dark night" back to Kansas City and the Rockhurst dorms.

A footnote: I think the leader's mother purchased the strips of blue velvet that were sewn on the lapels of white sportscoats. A bit clever if you think about it.

E. PLAYING THE KAY ELECTRIC IN "THE SLIM AND CURLY SHOW" IN THE ROCKHURST VARIETY SHOW.

The Slim and Curly Show at Rockhurst

Ahem, those are American Eagles on my cowboy boots. This was indeed one of the most fun, entertaining moments of the Guitar Music Odyssey. I've written extensively about it in "Coming of Age with the Jesuits," but want to give it a full-blown treatment in this narrative. Pardon me, the photo tells it all. It was marvelous. I am not sure of the "genesis" but am sure it came from a lot of horsing around with music during Junior Year at Rockhurst. Aside from my aspirations with Classic Guitar, I still had the old Kay and Amplifier, and we horsed around in my dorm room up on the hill at Sedgewick Hall, me playing and singing, and joined by soon to be best buddy Bill Rost of Jefferson City, Missouri. What we eventually came up with was a raucous parody of country music for the annual perhaps big city "stuffy" Rockhurst Variety Show. Some background.

It was called "Slim and Curly's Noontime Jamboree" and was based on a real 30-minute country music radio show from KSAL in Salina, Kansas, a show I must have listened to regularly over a couple of years. I know it came on at noon time, so I was probably in the farmhouse having dinner and a break from farm work for Dad. The show was called "Country Jamboree" with local talent from Salina and area; I don't recall but there was probably a rhythm guitar, a lead guitar, and for sure a fiddle and maybe drums. I don't think these guys were ready for the Grand Ole Opry, and I for sure was not that big a fan of country music (already explained). But Bill and I would incorporate all the parts of that show, make fun of them all, and I somewhere have the one page, ragged, torn original script at home. Scanned black and white page copies appear below. So, I guess you can accurately say the original idea came from me, but it was Bill's talent, stage presence, ability to harmonize and corny humor that made it a jewel. I would give anything to have a video of that performance. We played it to standing ovations at the annual Rockhurst Variety Shows.

WILD WILL CRICK   SINGIN SLIM SANDERS

KREA RADIO, SWEET SPRINGS, MO.

1. Howdedoo

2. Greetings

3. Romantic ballad: His and hers   beings a month ance Valentines Day

   There's a house, where they lived, his and hers
   The garage, with two cars, his and hers
   On their hands, matching bands, his and hers
   In their home, two telephones, his and hers

   On the table, two coffeycups, his and hers
   In the Den, two easy chairs, his and hers
   On the outside, looking in, all is well
   On the inside, there's a story, too sad to tell

   Two pillers, in separate rooms, his and hers
   Love was in sight, did one love die, his or hers
   Who's at fault, is their love lost, his or hers

4. Will, pulls himself together while I read the market report.

   Kansas City: 3000 hogs, 2000 sheep, 14000 cattle, consignment from Ted
                 Glutz up near Saolan for 200 head of Herford steers.
                 Hogs- 13   Steers-18
   Chicago: 4000 hogs, 5000 sheep, 18,000 cattle, hogs-13, cattle 15

5. Advertisement, Gooch feed
     Freinds and neightbors, as you know the Gooch feed company of Salina Kansas
     is bring you this here program. Gooch makes ffed for hoghs, cattle, sheep,
     horses, geese, ducks, chickens, capons, dogs, cats. You name it, we got
     it.
        Got a whole new line of household feeds: pancake mix, waffle mix, and
        flour mix. But the special thing is this new psychologically developed
        baby food.   Called ps-3   Designed to avoid bed wetting, temper
        tantrums, crying over spilt milk, and stuffy that that.   Doesn't have
        any drugs, barbituates, nicotine, or caffein. (also doesn't have
        any vitamins, proteins, fats, carbohydrates, or that stuff either.)
        But what it does have is that psychological effect to make the fat
        rool on.   Pick it up at your handy Gooch store in the handy 50
        lb. bag.   diddly durned

6. Speaking of babies, got a letter.   Baby of the day.

        There's a new arrival in town today.
        A new, little baby boy.
        I'm praying that he'll b a good one.
        Our little baby Sonny Kuntz.
                        we doin a babos eduation !!! you

7. Advertisement: Jed Longhoofer over in Industry Kansas has 14 weanling
                   pigs to sell. Says he hasn't been able to get rid of them,
                   so he'll take about anything he can get.
                   (I wonder what he means by that?)

        Sow joke

8. Dirty L'l

158

9. Time to quit feeling around that have the next song: Roundhouse, screen

18¼

    Movin On.

Ole Hound dog was feelin fine
till he fell in the vat of turpentine
He's movin on, He'll soon be gone
He passed the gate like an 88, He's movin on

Old tome cat was feelin mean
till he caught his tail in the sewing machine
he's movin on, He'll soon be gone
Ripped a stitch when he hit that ditch, He's moving on.

Man from the city saw a stripped kitty
Picked it up cause it was might pretty
He's movin on, He'll soon be gone
We held our nose as we burned his clothes, He's moving on

   Guitar

Hired a man to work on my car
Grabbed a hold of the spark plug wire
He's movin on, He'll soon be gone
He let loose when he felt the juice, he's moving on

Grampa Amos was feeling keen
Until he fell in the washing machine
He's movin on, He'll soon be gone
He just can't straddle that doggoned paddle, he's moving on

10. Spiritual, a new one, The Great Speckled Bird, First time in public
      (second ever)

185

F¹

What a beautiful thought I am thinking
Concerning the great speckled bird
Remember her name is recorded
on the pages of God's holy Word.

I am glad I have learned of her meekness
I am glad that my name's on the book
I want to be one never fearing
On the face of my saviour to look

When He cometh descending from Heaven
On a cloud, as is writ in the Word
I'll be carried right up there to meet him
On the wings of the great speckled bird

Don't look for no eagle
all this is in a speckled bird.

11. Good byek - thought for the day
   Friends, if Slim and me and all of you out there in the audience
  would live as the good book tells us we ought to live, we could be
 sure there would be good weather ahead in that eternal flight to heaven.

MUDY DOO
MOUTAIN DEW
JUST A CLOSER WALK WITH THEE
CATTLE CALL
TUMBLIN TUMBLEWEEDS
COOL WATER

As you can see above, there was a theme song to start us off and some old classics (note; the program changed slightly in its second year) like Hank Thompson's "I'm Moving On." We played "The Mom and Dad's Waltz" for anniversaries; requests were always called or mailed in. "Keep those cards and letters coming, folks." Then came a birthday song, and there was always a spiritual at the end, generally "Just a Closer Walk with Thee." We were in tune, most of the time, me singing melody and Bill a pretty good harmonizer. But it was the "corny" jokes between us, the "palaverin' and the commercials that were the best.

The "business" side of the program was based on a real phenomenon growing up on the farm a mile outside the city limits of Abilene, Kansas. Gooch Best Feeds was a major source of prepared livestock feed sold in 50 lb. paper bags. Each bag had a red circle worth points of course. You cut out the circles, kept them and when you had enough you could go to the annual Gooch Best Livestock Sale on a beautiful ranch in the hills west of Salina, Kansas for the auction. I never did have enough circles to matter much but did attend the auction once with a friend and we ate lots of free hot dogs and drank soda pop.

So, our sponsor for the parody was Gooch's Best, and we sold cattle feed, hog feed, chicken feed and even baby feed, egging on the audience to save those red circle points. The show was full of letters (hilariously made up by Bill most of the time) from our radio audience. This was one of my happiest moments at Rockhurst, not just the successful shows themselves, but all those Saturday mornings in the dorm when we would practice, I surmise driving roommate Denny Noonan and buddies crazy. But they seemed to enjoy it too. I played an electric guitar (the Kay) with a small amplifier and Bill just sang. What a memory!

F. PLAYING FIFTEEN MINUTES OF CLASSIC GUITAR AT THE VARIETY SHOW

MY ONLY TRUE "CONCERT" EXPERIENCE

The other experience for the Variety Show was a one-time thing. I played solo, a short set of classic guitar pieces, for about fifteen minutes to a large crowd, perhaps of two or three hundred persons. It was the closest yours truly would ever come to a true classic guitar concert. Amazing was it went extremely well; there was loud and long applause when it was finished. Most amazing was the performance gratefully was not affected by serious nerves or stage fright; the fingers worked properly as did the memory. I am grateful yet today, perhaps sixty years later for that moment. As I will end this narrative with a reference to an imagined classic guitar concert, this one evening is the inspiration.

G. POST ROCKHURST GRADUATION – THE SUMMER OF 1963

THE 50 -50 CLUB FOR 10 WEEKS

This is a huge chapter in the music odyssey. I had received a **NDEA** (National Defense Education Act) full-ride fellowship to Saint Louis University for the coming semester to begin work on a **Ph.D.** in Spanish and Latin American Studies, so there was no big worry about finances come September. On a whim I decided to "beat the bushes" for a place to play music. Someone mentioned the 50-50 Club just a few blocks from Rockhurst; I think we must have drunk some beer there the preceding year.

So I took a deep breath, walked in and talked to the Italian owner and offered my services. Who knows why he accepted, but the jist was I would play six nights a week, from 8 o'clock to midnight for $50 dollars a week and all the Italian food I could eat. Oh, an aside: the **ASCAP** people were active in Kansas City because of all the bars and nightclubs, the Union people who required a union card as a "license" to play. The owner of the club just said, "No problem. Don't worry, I'll take care of it." No further mention of that union card ever took place.

An aside. I do not know if my boss had an affiliation with a certain underworld group in Kansas City, but perhaps, just perhaps, that was how he fixed it. I did learn later that the joint had burned down three separate times over the years, always rebuilt. It must have been the insurance money, do you think?

So as Ed Sullivan would say, "Away we go." I would play all those nights for about two months of the summer. The instrument was the Sears – Roebuck classic, no amplifier, but the 50-50 club had a raised platform in one corner of the bar and a good microphone that would pick up both the guitar and my voice. I recall there was a shelf to the side and that one night I had at least six glasses of beer bought by the customers waiting to keep my throat wet. Ha! I am sure I never drank to the point of being drunk; you couldn't play and sing in that shape, but I am sure I was feeling no pain.

You may wonder, where did I bunk? Brother Jim was working in Kansas City at the time for an elevator manufacturing company and rented a small house on the Kansas side, so I was invited to move in and make myself at home. I do recall driving to that tiny house each night at about 1 a.m.

Back to the music. And the crowd in the bar. A few of the former buddies at Rockhurst were regulars, so I had a bit of a cheering section. And there were many customers I of course did not know. But what made the whole gig enjoyable was a contingent of Peace Corps Volunteers who were training at the nearby branch of the University of Missouri in Kansas City. After long, arduous days of area studies and a cram course in Spanish language, they would all troop over to the bar. They arrived at about 9 p.m. and would stay until closing time. It was the era of "hootenanny" folk music, so I played folk music, singing, and I think some early learned country music, but I played songs in Spanish for that group. I do recall that very late I would play a set of classic guitar selections. I would like to include in this narration the lists of those songs; it is long. I recall learning about 200 new songs that summer. I would work on them during the daytime at Jim's house and try them out those nights. A list is a list, but each song is a memory and part of the Guitar Odyssey.

FOLK SONGS

1. The Green Leaves of Summer
2. Green, Green
3. All My sorrows
4. Blow the candle out
5. Shady Grove
6. Lonesome Traveler
7. Everglades
8. Scotch and Soda
9. The Seine
10. Tom Dooley
11. Scarlet Ribbons
12. Take her out of pity
13. Taste of honey
14. Three jolly coachmen
15. Tijuana Jail
16. Today
17. Greenback Dollar
18. Greensleeves
19. The Blue Tailed Fly
20. Corey
21. It was a very good year
22. Shenandoah
23. Denver
24. Sloop John B
25. Island in the Sun
26. Jamaica Farewell

27. Wayfaring Stranger
28. A worried man
29. There is a tavern in the town
30. This Land is your land
31. Minuet
32. Have some madeira, my dear
33. House of the Rising Sun

SONGS IN SPANISH

1. Ya es muy tarde
2. Peregrina
3. Las mañanitas
4. Malagueña salerosa
5. Allá en el rancho grande
6. Coplas (canción chistosa de doble sentido)
7. Guantanamera
8. Adelita
   (Later, In retirement, for information only for Christina's in Durango, learned from Linda Ronstadt's "Canciones de Mi Padre")
9. El adiós del soldado
10. Jalisco
11. La Llorona
12. La Barca de Guaymas
13. Granito de Sal
14. Hay unos ojos
15. Y ándale

FOR INFORMATION ONLY, BRAZILIAN SONGS AFTER BRAZIL

16. Mulher rendeira
17. O vento
18. O canoeiro

19. Manhã de Carnaval

All good (?) things have to end. The real first cause was the Peace Corps Training Program came to an end and off they went to Honduras. My college buddies still came around some, but most of the customers were the bar flies. And I was tired and "burning out." The second catalyst was when brother Jim came in one night, said, "I'm going fishing this weekend down in the Ozarks. Do you want to come along?" In milli-seconds, I picked up the guitar and put it in its case, gave a friendly, oral resignation to the boss, and that ended this first but not last foray into the entertainment world.

I think I ate mainly pizza but did have moments with a blond waitress on the Italian Restaurant side of the bar.

5

THE ACADEMIC TIMES CHANGE – ST. LOUIS - THE GUITAR GOES ALONG – 1963 TO 1966

That September of 1963 I was off to St. Louis, Missouri, and serious academics in the Ph.D. program. Most expenses were covered by the NDEA Grant: tuition, books, a single room in the dormitory, cafeteria food, and some spending money for beer, dates once in a while with a cute BSBA-Nursing School girl and keeping an old wreck of a car going. The car must have been from working 60 hours a week at the ice plant in summers in Abilene. It was a Ford 1957 Fairlane, blue and white, but just barely running. Before Brazil in 1966 I took it to the old one-armed negro mechanic on Pine Street and he just shook his head. The car limped along that Spring before I gave it to the Cusack girls when I left St. Louis for Brazil in 1966. They said later, "It died on us."

Music for those three years. First of all, there must have been the constant practice of classic pieces and maybe singing of folk songs in the privacy of my room in that first dorm room next to Griesedieck Hall. And then there were the great student parties where I would always take the guitar and we would sing the folk songs and I would play some classic. I do not recall well today 55 years later, but the hosts may have been

Sue Mailou, (French) Jeannie Giese, (English) Jo Anne and Tori Cusack, (Spanish) Carol Caufield, (Nursing) Martha Arms, (don't know). I met one Keah Runshang much later at one of those parties, probably in 1968. I played the guitar, we sang, the girls could harmonize. And good friend Dan Hayes in a monotone voice would do Folsom Prison Blues. There was much group dancing, a long line dance to Zorba the Greek we all loved. Today, knowing Liam Clancy's "Those were the days," it would have been perfect for that group.

The guys are all in the photo below, chosen because it is the only one I have of the Sears – Roebuck Classic:

The Sears – Roebuck Classic and the Student Party

Other than Dan, the other faces are familiar but only known to me is Bill Bockelman front row right and his brother third from left on the back row (Bill was instrumental in my first visit to St. Louis and days after). I'm not here to retell St. Louis days (they are in the Jesuit book) but the music at these parties was constant and important. Great memories.

And here is an old, sorry, fuzzy picture of all those great girls and guys:

Guys and Gals at Saint Louis University

In the back row, head just showing is good friend Luis Negrete of Mexico City (and the Philharmonic Orchestra) a welcome addition to our group for his music and our Spanish conversations. He was studying Medicine at Saint Louis University. It might have been this night when Luis and I after many "cervezas" wrote jointly our own "corrido" with all the filthy words we knew in Spanish.

Yo soy Felipe Bermejo
El que robó tanto amor
Y cuando vino el sherife
Casí murí de terror.

Pinche sherife pendejo
Chinga tu madre cabrón

Eres un hijo de puta
E comes caca cabrón..

Back to the dorm practice. Something very important happened my third year at St. Louis U.: I was housed in the graduate dorm at the old, converted Coronado Hotel on Lindell Blvd. All is fuzzy, but I think it was the place Harry Truman had his governor's inaugural ball before that all important surprise in 1948 when he defeated Thomas Dewey for the presidency.

Anyway, the place was fancy, "old" elegant, our dorm rooms spacious, a bit old fashioned but comfortable. But the lobby of the old Coronado was a sight to see: all in highly polished may I say "rococó" wood; wood paneled walls, short, ornate wooden railings, and the carved wooden columns all about. It was there on many a night I would repeat all the nights in the basement of Loyola-Xavier Hall Dormitory at Rockhurst in Kansas City, but in this incredibly elegant setting: the quiet practice of classic guitar pieces on the Sears- Roebuck. (I won't repeat the acute appendicitis attack that took place there and medical students rushed me to SLU Hospital for emergency surgery).

One other music memory suffices for those days. As usual, I hung out with the Latinos in order to practice Spanish (it was in the Griesedieck Hall lobby where I was talking with them that a boy from Panama rushed in one November morning in 1963 saying, "They shot President Kennedy"). We went to a real greasy spoon café down on Olive Street, past the "queer bar" as it was known in those days, on the corner. A heavy-set Mexican ran the café with his wife, and the food was tacos, enchiladas, etc. but the beer was icy cold (Busch Bavarian for my budget, or Budweiser if you had more money). But there was a jukebox and it had Mexican "rancheros" etc. One night I took my guitar to the place and played my very limited repertoire of Mexican Songs. A buddy from Tegucigalpa loved the "Comparsita" and I probably played "Malagueña" and some flamenco. I take note that the Latino friendships at SLU were fine, but never as life changing as the great experiences at Rockhurst with Eduardo Matheu and Brazilian Henrique Kerti.

In 1966 Spring I learned I had won a Fulbright-Hays Graduate Research Grant to Brazil to study its literature and the "Literatura de Cordel." Buddy Dan Hays, on a pure lark, applied to Portugal and won also. The difference was Dan really just wanted to get to Paris and the rest of Europe. Me, I made it to the beaches of Bahia and Rio and the backlands of the Northeast and took the whole thing a lot more seriously. Music is a minor chapter that year, coming up.

6

THE BRAZILIAN EXPERIENCE – 1966 TO 1967

I have written elsewhere and often of that life-changing experience. See "Adventures of a 'Gringo' Researcher in Brazil in the 1960s – In Search of the 'Literatura de Cordel.'" Music was not the priority.

One word sums up Brazilian music in the 1960s: "samba." There were many variants, "baião" in Pernambuco, samba in Salvador da Bahia, but mainly the samba of Rio de Janeiro and its carnival parades, plus the samba played by a "Golden Age" of Brazilian pop musicians in Rio, São Paulo and the national TV song festivals. A future hero and personage of many books was Chico Buarque de Hollanda. One almost never heard of classical guitar musicians in Brazil; there were some, but not many. I met one in the Rio de Janeiro Airport, o Galeão, with his guitar in his case on the way to a concert tour; we chatted for just a moment, perhaps Mr. Barbosa? (Their greatest, Laurindo Almeida, skipped the country, ended up in Los Angeles and became famous in both classic and jazz and movie soundtrack worlds. His good buddy who studied classic with him in Brazil ended up playing samba on the radio!).

But there was a samba variant which dominated my memories: Bossa Nova and especially the music in the film "Orféu Negro" ["Black Orpheus"] by Luís de Bonfá .

In the early research days in the northeast in June of 1966 living in an "ateliê" of art in Olinda, Pernambuco, I heard and participated a bit in quiet Brazilian – stye "serenatas" on the street curbs and sidewalks of those old 400-year-old "sobrados" of this famous colonial city. There, Brazilian friends would strum the nylon string guitars, play "samba" or "baiao." Now we are down to Brass Tacks: I never did get the "hang" of the samba rhythm, and just learned one or two songs, "Mulher Rendeira" and later "Manhã de Carnival," neither of which I played well. Brazilians say gringos can't dance samba; I totally agree (except when really "oiled up'" with Brazilian Beer). For sure they can't play samba. Except for Allan Sandomir at ASU. My Portuguese language student Allan was trained in classic guitar but had a love for Brazilian music, went to Brazil and absorbed the whole milieu. He started a very successful samba band during his classes with me in Portuguese and the band became a mainstay for Carnival. I've heard Allan play many of the famous Bossa Nova hits and Fernando Sor "estudios" as well. One of my most memorable students, but the samba did not wear off on me.

There is however a very happy ending to Brazil in 1966-1967 for me. A DiGiorgio Classic Guitar. I knew before leaving for Brazil in June of 1966 that the country produced fine rosewood classic guitars, but the idea was just vague about getting one. Happenstance allowed me to live frugally for five months in Recife in the colorful "Chácara das Rosas" boarding house for young men. The important note was it cost USD $ 35 per month, room and board, albeit scanty meals. In Bahia in November, I moved up to much more costly but still reasonable housing in "A Portuguesa" boarding house [pensão]. Result: I had saved some money with the idea of buying the instrument.

Fate or something led me to "A Guitarra da Prata" store on the Rua do Carioca in downtown Rio that December. It probably sold all kinds of musical instruments, but I saw only "violões" – guitars. My knowledge of brands and makes was zilch, but it turns out the classic guitar makers were all Italian, the instruments made in the shops of greater São Paulo.

DiGiorgio, Giannini and Del Vecchio. They were displayed hanging carefully from racks in the store, and for the finer guitars, in closed wooden closets.

The other moment of "fortuna" as author O'Toole of "A Confederation of Dunces" might say, was something good for the Brazilians and good for me: the economy was in the doldrums, so the "Guitarra da Prata" was offering huge discounts *if you paid in cash!* I picked out a gorgeous rosewood DiGiorgio and was offered a quiet place in the glass enclosed "tryout" room of the store. Naturally, the acoustics were just right for such an occasion. The guitar fretted beautifully, and the tone was nothing like I had ever experienced. And the darned thing was beautiful: Brazilian rosewood sides and back, another fine wood on the neck, ebony keyboard and etc. for the top. The tuning keys were mother of pearl enclosed in what looked like a gold finish. Here are the pictures:

The DiGiorgio with Decals on Its Case

The DiGiorgio in its case, years later, adorned with decals from my travel world. Credit classic guitarist Siegfried Behrund from Germany whose case gave me the idea at the University of Missouri, Kansas City, concert perhaps in 1962.

The DiGiorgio in All Its Glory

So, I took my accumulated cash savings from Recife and Bahia and bought the guitar. That day I did a rare thing and hired a taxi to go "home" to my hosts' house in Flamengo, cradling the instrument in the back seat like a newborn baby. I later asked my hosts to "guard" the guitar while I continued research trips in Brazil. The final chapter in Brazil in 1967 was the battle with the steward or stewardesses of Pan American Airlines on the flight home from Rio to New York in maybe July of 1967 to allow me to place the guitar in its case in the small "suit" closet up front in the airplane. They insisted it go in luggage where surely it would have cracked; my persistence carried the day.

A footnote: after several years in the dry heat of Arizona, the guitar did begin to have slight surface cracks on the top, and two or three more serious on the side, to the bottom. I found an amazing artisan in downtown Phoenix who fixed it all, taught me how to use humidifiers in the guitar, and it remains fixed and beautiful and PLAYABLE to this day.

As mentioned, any learning of pieces in Brazil was at a minimum, but began again in Abilene, Kansas at my parents' house while writing the Ph.D. dissertation in the fall of 1967 and spring of 1968. Serious study and growth of the classical repertoire would be in Tempe, Arizona where a new chapter of life continued with the job as Assistant Professor of Spanish beginning in the Fall of 1968 and continuing into formal retirement in 2002 and part-time for some years later.

7

ABILENE, THE DISSERTATION,
ST. LOUIS, AND ON TO
ARIZONA – 1967 TO 1969

After returning from Brazil in July of 1967, there was one thing on my mind: writing the dissertation for the Ph.D. The original plan was to live in the upstairs rooms of my parents' house on Rogers Street in Abilene, Kansas, organize the material and do the writing. Memories are vague, but I know I spent most daytimes in a tiny room filled with cigarette smoke, organizing and writing. I sent the first two or three chapters to my advisor at Saint Louis University that Fall. An aside is permitted (told in other books). Things had evolved or changed since classroom days at St. Louis U. My terrific professor and mentor of Portuguese and Brazilian Literature had moved on, now a Professor of Portuguese and Latin American Studies at Kent State University. Her successor was a highly professional, deeply involved person, cognizant of Literary Criticism, and he imagined my dissertation on Brazilian folk and popular poetry to be like those of lyric poetry. One and two don't make four. My chapters were criticized, I mistakenly called him "pedantic," and the Jesuit head of the Modern Languages Program threatened to throw me out of the program.

The erudite Portuguese professor declined to continue as director, so Father Rosario Mazza took over, but with stipulations. Shape up! After a long ordeal trying to survive in St. Louis living at good friend Dan Hayes' parents' house in Maplewood and substitute teaching in St. Louis, I managed another chapter or two, had good friend Jeannie Giese of the English Department correct my English and type the "opus." I had a very brief Ph.D. Dissertation done in June 1968. (When queried why it was so short, I could only say, "That's all I had to say.") Today my writings might be 6000 pages.

Why all this? Because back in Abilene in the fall of 1967 and Spring of 1968, I surely played classic music on the DiGiorgio and got together with old friend Eddy Smith and bongo artist Bob Hensley to play some folk, pop, and rock music. In St. Louis in the final months, I played the guitar at the Modern Language Department student parties and there met Miss Keah Runshang.

Skip to September 1968, me ensconced in an apartment in Tempe, Arizona, rookie assistant professor of Spanish at ASU. One of the first guitar memories was when invited to one of those social get togethers for ASU faculty, which meant drinks (beer in my case) and dinner, I was asked to play some classic guitar. I obliged, pulling out the DiGiorgio and proceeded to play the "Six Lute Pieces of the Renaissance" (in D), but introduced them with a pithy statement, "Ring the snot out of it, Jake!" I played the suite well, amazingly all six pieces memorized, and the host couple, proper New Englanders, seemed to enjoy it. My friends Philip and Mary Leonard never forgot the moment and would remind now again years later, laughing and laughing.

It was in those years, from the first bachelor year to years of marriage to Keah Runshang, that Gammage Auditorium at Arizona State University contributed in no small way to "Guitars and Music." The lesser way first: no less than Johnny Cash, his wife June, and Marty Robbins all performed at a single concert. Marty Robbins' "A White Sport Coat" from high school days and the great "El Paso" were among my country favorites.

Johnny Cash with "Folsom Prison Blues," "I'll Walk the Line" and of course he and June singing "We Got Married in a Fever" are memories. But a singular "down" memory of that memorable concert was that the country hicks in Arizona booed Marty Robbins in their haste to hear Cash. I'll never forget it.

Of far greater consequence over the years and always moments to encourage Curran the amateur classical guitarist was first, a concert by Carlos Montoya, the flamenco master of the times, then Julian Bream, renowned Lutenist, Andrés Segovia, the uncontested "first chair" of classical guitarists, and then the "Royal Family of the Guitar" (Los Romeros). Much later there was no less than Christopher Parkening with concert and master class.

Montoya inspired me to purchase at Milano Music in Mesa a single book with perhaps six to ten of his flamenco solos. It is a given you cannot learn to play decent flamenco from that, but by listening to and wearing out a 33rpm record with the same songs, I managed to do a weak facsimile of flamenco. Three I can play yet today:

Huelva. Montoya
Zapateado, Montoya
La Zambra, Montoya.

If you add my toned-down version of "Malagueña" you get 15 minutes of music like it might come from Spain. Aside from the rapid plucking with the right hand, the real key is the "rasgueado," perhaps the correct term, a keynote of flamenco style. The Caves of Granada were not present in Tempe, Arizona, but I gave it my best. Let's see: you strum the chord beginning with a closed right fist, then successively with all four fingers of the right hand, first finger to little finger, 1,2,3,4 and then back, 4,3,2,1. And all very quickly. An added feature, when you can work it in, is between "strums," tap the guitar with your thumb, keeping the rhythm. Wow am I impressing myself! Ha ha. Not really. But it sounds okay.

Important, extremely important: this imitation of Carlos Montoya and the classical masters to come over the last 55 years is what do you say? Pro and con, good and bad, positive and negative. I think all musicians, professional, semi-professional and amateur must go through it:

On the one hand, you are incredibly inspired by the masters and do all you can to imitate them.

On the other hand, you never can reach that level of mastery. It all ends being what I call a "facsimile," and there are times when one says, "Forget it. I can' do it." I have many classic records from 33 rpm days, tapes, and now CDs. On occasion I listen to them with pleasure and some doubt because of the above. But it is the music of those masters that INSPIRES, CHALLENGES and sometimes SUCCEEDS IN GREAT SATISFACTION. Now in my early 80s, with arthritis affecting my play, the re-fretting of old learned positions, and playing ever more slowly, all that I have said and remember is true.

Talent, motivation and perseverance. I cannot fathom the true professionals, knowing that eight hours of practice a day for years with good instructors is probably the norm. How they do it. How do they persist? The reward I am sure is the applause of their audiences, but I suspect it is also sitting quietly playing the classics with great élan, this perhaps without an audience or teacher. I may come back to this.

A second moment was a single Julian Bream concert, wonderful! See the program:

GAMMAGE CENTER *for the* PERFORMING ARTS

1972-1973 SEASON

Art of the Guitar Series
by arrangement with HAROLD SHAW

presents

JULIAN BREAM

Lutenist & Guitarist

Sunday, March 25, 1973   3:00 p.m.

PROGRAM

I
Lute

Branle - Air de Court - Wolte (1603) .... JEAN BAPTISTE BESARD
(1567-d?)

Fantasia (1610) .... GREGORIO HUWETT

Ricecar .... FRANCESCO DA MILANO
La Canzon delli Ucelli
Fantasia
Ricecar: La Compagna
(1497-1543)

Pavan .... WILLIAM BYRD
The Woods So Wild
(1543-1623)

Intermission

II
Guitar

Sonata in A minor .... J. S. BACH
(1685-1750)

    Prelude
    Fugue
    Siciliano
    Presto

Overture in A, Opus 61 .... MAURO GIULIANI
(1781-1840)

Bagatelles (1972) .... WILLIAM WALTON
(B. 1902)

Three Spanish Pieces .... JOAQUIN TURINA
(1882-1947)

    Fandanguillo
    Soleares
    Rafaga

RCA RECORDS
Management: SHAW CONCERTS, INC., 233 West 49th Street, N.Y. 10019

A third model was the greatest of them all, Andrés Segovia (I mean for traditional classic guitar). I had the good fortune to hear him only once but never forgotten, at Gammage Auditorium. I was accompanied by good friend, lutenist and guitarist, Frank Farmer. We took our programs backstage, stood in awe in front of the master and got his autograph.

His program that night:

Arizona State University
Gammage Center for the Performing Arts

presents

ANDRES SEGOVIA

guitar

I. Two Pieces (1538) . . . . L. de Narvaez

   Suite in d minor . . . . R. de Visee (1650-1725)

   Siciliana . . . . J. S. Bach (1685-1750)
   Fuga
   Gavotta

Pause

II. Berceuse d'Orient . . . . Al. Tansman (b. 1897)
   Danza Pomposa

   Sonata Mexicana . . . . M. Ponce (1882-1948)
     Allegretto
     Intermezzo
     Andante
     Allegro

   Tarantella . . . . M. Castelnuovo-Tedesco (1895-1968)

INTERMISSION

III. Dance in E . . . . E. Granados (1867-1916)
   Dance in G
   Tonadilla

   Leyenda . . . . I. Albeniz (1860-1909)

RAMIREZ GUITAR   RCA, DECCA/MCA RECORDS

EXCLUSIVE MANAGEMENT: ICM Artists, Ltd.
40 West 57th Street, New York, N.Y. 10019
Sheldon Gold, President
(An MJA Services Company)

A note on the performance. The stage was empty save for a single straight-backed chair (at least with a padded seat), a wooden footstool, and a stage mike (I think) a few feet in front. Segovia walks out on stage to enthusiastic applause, sits on the chair, and has to rock back and forth, using his left foot (I surmise because of his age), to get the damned footstool exactly in place where he wants it; it seems he can't bend over safely. Then for perhaps 90 minutes we are entertained. As I say, the entire program was of the "official" master composers for Classic guitar.

The biographical note:

ANDRES SEGOVIA

In January, 1978 Andres Segovia celebrated the fiftieth anniversary of his first appearance in the United States.

No noticeable change accompanied this impressive date — as always, his concerts were sold-out and stages were crammed with seats. As always, critics around the world re-echoed the words of Albert Goldberg writing in the Los Angeles Times: "Andres Segovia's guitar playing is one of the miracles of our time."

Andres Segovia was born in Linares, a village in southern Spain. His father, an attorney, hoped Andres would follow in the same career. To broaden the youngster's cultural background, he provided the boy with piano lessons. Andres, however, rebelled having discovered a guitar in the home of a friend. Attempts to have the boy learn a "respectable" instrument like the violin or cello also failed. Andres, enchanted by the guitar, decided "for better or worse" to make it his career.

Objections from his family and teachers at the Granada Institute of Music where he studied, proved to no avail. Segovia was determined to succeed as a serious artist with an instrument that had never been accorded a place on the concert stage. Unable to find a capable instructor, Segovia became his own guide. "To this day," he says with a twinkle in his eye, "teacher and pupil have never had a serious quarrel."

He made his first public appearance in Granada at the age of fourteen. His debut, sponsored by a local cultural organization, the Circula Artistico, was described as a "revelation." Within a short time his name was known throughout Spain. At the age of twenty-two, Segovia appeared at the Paris Conservatory. His success resulted in an extensive concert tour.

In 1919 Segovia's appearance in South America proved to be a sensation. He did not return to Europe until 1923. At that time, many persons attended Segovia's concerts because they expected a novelty, but they came back to admire and cheer. The critic of the London "Times" confessed, "In the fullness of our ignorance we went, expecting we did not know what, but hoping since Senor Segovia's reputation had preceded him and the name of Johann Sebastian Bach appeared on his program, that we would satisfy our curiosity about an instrument that had romantic associations, without being outraged musically. We remained to hear the last possible note, for it was the most delightful surprise of the season!"

Leading composers began to write for the guitarist, among them Alfredo Casella and Mario Castelnuovo-Tedesco who composed concertos dedicated to Segovia. In January, 1928, the virtuoso, still unknown in the United States, arrived in New York for his debut at Town Hall. Olin Downes in the New York Times reported: "He belongs to the very small group of musicians who by transcendent powers of execution and imagination create an art of their own, and sometimes seem to transform the very nature of their medium."

Segovia's was the first guitar recital in New York. Within five years he had achieved a record of six completely sold-out New York concerts. In the next eleven weeks he played forty American engagements.

In 1943, Segovia first began his transcontinental tours of the United States and Canada under the direction of impresario Sol Hurok. Since then he has also appeared as soloist with a number of major symphony orchestras.

With a small orchestra background in January, 1946, Segovia gave his first concert at Carnegie Hall. Virgil Thomson, critic of the New York Herald Tribune commented: "There is no guitar but the Spanish guitar and Andres Segovia is its prophet. I doubt if there lives a music lover with soul so dead that he could not find reward in attendance at a Segovia concert."

Segovia concerts continue to guarantee sold-out houses around the globe. The New York Times once noted that: "Andres Segovia's affection for the guitar and the music he finds to play on it seems to remain as constant as the public that flocks to hear him whenever he gives a concert."

In addition to Castelnuovo-Tedesco and Casella, the guitarist has had works dedicated to him by Alexander Tansman, Manuel deFalla, Heitor Villa-Lobos, Manuel Ponce, Albert Roussel, Jacques Ibert, Cyril Scott and Frederico Torroba.

A benign old-world gentleman, Andres Segovia usually wears string ties or flowing ribbon ones. He lives with his wife part of the year in Madrid and Switzerland, and the other months tours extensively in the United States, Europe and South America, pausing often to visit old friends along the way. Far Eastern audiences continually request a visit.

A gracious heart and a charming conversationalist, Andres Segovia, even in the bustle of New York, seems surrounded by the poise and courtesy of a more elegant, more gracious world.

Then the critic's note:

D2

He still knows how to turn a phrase in a way that can make your heart stop

Segovia projects brilliance despite the march of time

By Dimitri Drobatschewsky
Special for The Republic

ANDRES SEGOVIA
Guitar. Arizona State University Gammage Center, Thursday.

An outburst of affection greeted Andres Segovia, the grand old man of the classical guitar, the moment he appeared on the stage of Gammage Center. The capacity audience showered him with one ovation after another, between selections, at intermission, and at the conclusion of his recital Thursday night.

Segovia's prestige and reputation as classical guitarist have been built over more than five decades, and today, old and young audiences alike revere this unique artist. It is he who put J.S. Bach on the musical map outside of his traditional setting, with transcriptions for classical guitar that sound more "genuine" than their original versions. Composers of all origins used to vie for the privilege to compose for Segovia: Thus one of the most beautiful concertos for guitar was created by Mario Castelnuovo-Tedesco and has become solidly entrenched in the standard repertoire.

But, for a number of years, time has begun to take its toll on the seemingly immortal Segovia. For one, the volume of sound that he produces has become smaller and smaller. At times it is quite difficult to hear him, especially when the attention span of the audience begins to lag. Also, the fire and verve has gone out of some of his interpretations, and his tone colorations have become a little monotonous. Too much of the same, perhaps, and no longer played with the utterly imaginative creativeness that was once Segovia's trademark.

He still knows how to turn a phrase in a way that can make your heart stop. In two *Danzas* by Enrique Granados, Segovia displayed the gracious elegance combined with the distinctive Spanish temperament that makes listening to his interpretation of Spanish guitar music unforgettable. He was equally seductive in Isaac Albeniz's *Leyenda*, a work that could be regarded as Segovia's theme song.

The early part of the program, devoted to 17th century composers de Visee and de Narvaez, did not ignite the audience, at least not until the only Bach pieces (*Siciliana*, *Fuga*, and *Gavotta*) were offered. Segovia still has no peer for Bach on the guitar, and the listeners knew it when they clapped and shouted their approval after the familiar *Fuga*.

Three selections by Alexandre Tansman, M. Ponce, and Castelnuovo-Tedesco found Segovia struggling a bit with intonation (he frequently tuned his guitar during quick rests), which caused the audience to become restless. Rustling of programs, squirming in seats and, finally, extensive coughing made listening to the soft sound projection a bit difficult. Those problems disappeared, however, during the final part of the concert.

There was, of course, a standing ovation at the end of the regular program. But when the last of the encores had faded away, the joy of having heard one of the world's greatest performing musicians play was mixed with a little bit of sadness at the passing of time and the fading of an artist who has for many years been a legend in the world of music.

Very different but perhaps more motivating in later years were two performances by "The Royal Family of the Guitar," the Romeros, Father and three sons, obviously forming a quartet, doing flamenco but mainly classic pieces. It was where I first heard the "6 Lute Pieces from the Renaissance" which I later learned.

The family fled Spain (Málaga) during the Franco regime when artists and musicians were considered "suspect" by the centrist government. Celedonio took the family eventually to Los Angeles, started the quartet and they became a great success.

The Program:

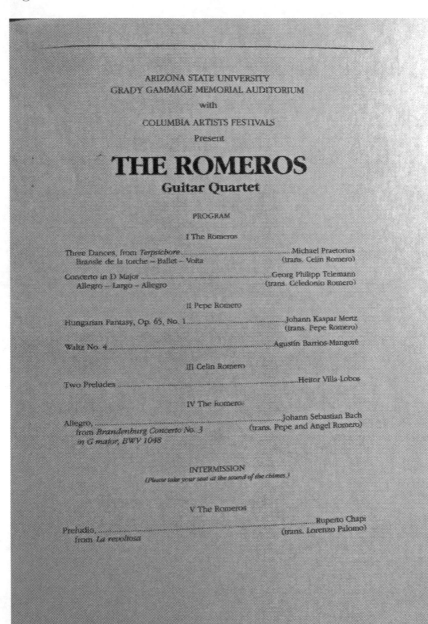

ARIZONA STATE UNIVERSITY
GRADY GAMMAGE MEMORIAL AUDITORIUM

with

COLUMBIA ARTISTS FESTIVALS
Present

THE ROMEROS
Guitar Quartet

PROGRAM

I The Romeros

Three Dances, from *Terpsichore* .... Michael Praetorius
Bransle de la torche – Ballet – Volta (trans. Celin Romero)

Concerto in D Major .... Georg Philipp Telemann
Allegro – Largo – Allegro (trans. Celedonio Romero)

II Pepe Romero

Hungarian Fantasy, Op. 65, No. 1 .... Johann Kaspar Mertz
(trans. Pepe Romero)

Waltz No. 4 .... Agustín Barrios-Mangoré

III Celin Romero

Two Preludes .... Heitor Villa-Lobos

IV The Romeros

Allegro, ... Johann Sebastian Bach
from *Brandenburg Concerto No. 3* (trans. Pepe and Angel Romero)
in G major, BWV 1048

INTERMISSION
(Please take your seat at the sound of the chimes.)

V The Romeros

Preludio, ... Ruperto Chapi
from *La revoltosa* (trans. Lorenzo Palomo)

VI Angel Romero

Introduction, Theme and Variations ....Fernando Sor
  on a Theme from Mozart's *The Magic Flute*

Sevilla ....Isaac Albéniz
  (trans. Angel Romero)

VII Celedonio Romero

Fantasia ....Celedonio Romero

VIII The Romeros

Miller's Dance ....Manuel de Falla
  from *El sombrero de tres picos*   (trans. Pepe Romero)

El baile de Luis Alonso ....Jerónimo Giménez
                                                                      (trans. Pepe Romero)

COLUMBIA ARTISTS FESTIVALS
a division of COLUMBIA ARTISTS MANAGEMENT INC.
HERBERT O. FOX / ROBERT KAY   ROBERT McCRILLIS
Associate: Susan Lamborghini   Booking Director: Richard DeSimone
4605 Lankershim Boulevard   Associate: Alexander Castonguay
North Hollywood, CA 91602   165 West 57th St. New York, NY 10019

PROGRAM NOTES

Three Dances from *Terpsichore*...Praetorius
                                                                      (1571-1621)

Michael Praetorius was a German composer, theorist, and organist. He is considered to
be the most versatile and wide-ranging German composer of his generation. Most of
the works in his vast output are vocal; *Terpsichore*, the most important of his
instrumental compositions, is a collection of dances taking its name from the Greek
muse of dance. Published in 1612, the historic collection contains harmonizations of a
great number of popular tunes from the court of Henry IV, three of which are
presented here.

Concerto in D major ....Telemann
                                                                      (1681-1767)

Telemann was considered one of the greatest German composers of his day and
enjoyed a popularity far greater than his friend and contemporary, Johann Sebastian
Bach. His list of compositions is so long as to preclude enumeration, and the
publication of his entire work is still far from complete; many of his works are still
being rediscovered. Especially noted as a highly skilled contrapuntalist, he wrote with
ease and fluency in all styles from opera and church music to instrumental works of
the greatest variety.

On another occasion, I heard the "6 Lute Pieces for the Renaissance" but do not have the program. This is impressionistic: Celedonio did the first of the lute pieces (of 6), then Celín, then Pepe and finally Ángel. My impressions: Celedonio was definitely in charge, and his claim to fame is he blended classic with flamenco in his own compositions. Celín was the oldest son, competent, but not flashy. I think he might have been 4th in the pecking order of talent and performance, but by no means shoddy. Pepe was and is my favorite, a true master of the guitar, a real "whiz" who could play brilliantly any of the masterpieces – "Leyenda," "Asturias," and those of Bach, Sor, or Villa Lobos. Ángel probably was just as good as Pepe, but later grew weary for whatever reason of the quartet and branched out as a conductor and solo artist. I have recordings of them all.

The Romeros, Biography

THE ROMEROS

To some fortunate musicians, it is given to rise to the peak of a musical art form; to some very few musicians, it is given to originate an art form. The Romeros have achieved both. In a recent lengthy article, The *New York Times* said: "Collectively, they are the only classical guitar quartet of real stature in the world today; in fact, they virtually invented the format."

The illustrious career of Celedonio Romero and his three sons – Celin, Pepe and Angel – is unmistakably a milestone of twentieth century music. The internationally renowned Spanish artists are known as "The Royal Family of the Guitar," for their virtuosity remains peerless in the music world today. Since they came to the United States in 1958, they have consistently dazzled audiences everywhere and have inspired enthusiastic praise from critics coast to coast. Whether performing as a quartet, trio, duo, or as soloists in recital, and with symphony orchestra, the Romeros prevail as champions in the realm of classical guitar.

Celedonio was a soloist in Franco's Spain. As each of his three sons reached the age of two or three, they began learning the guitar from their father. All three sons had made their debuts in Spain by the time they were seven years old. Finally in 1958, the family came to the United States where they began performing as a quartet while the sons were still in their teens. To have four virtuosi of the same instrument in one family is unique in the music world, and in the realm of the classical guitar it is absolutely without precedent. Each of the four is individually ranked as an internationally known soloist; joined together they produce music which is extraordinary.

As recognition for his contributions to Spanish culture, Celedonio Romero was recently presented with the highest civilian honor granted by His Majesty, the King of Spain, Don Juan Carlos I – *Commendador de Numero de La Orden de Isabel la Católica* ("Great Knight Commander of the Order of *Isabel la Católica*"). Then in the summer of 1989, Celedonio Romero and his entire family were honored in a week-long celebration and tribute from the city of Málaga, Spain, concurrent with the opening of the Celedonio Romero Foundation and Guitar Museum in that city. The sterling reputation of the Romeros has further been earned by repeated appearances with virtually every major symphony orchestra in the United States including those of Boston, Cleveland, Chicago, Philadelphia, Los Angeles, San Francisco, Pittsburgh, Detroit and many others. The family has twice been invited to perform at the White House, in 1983 they appeared at the Vatican in a special concert for Pope John II, and in 1986 they performed for His Royal Highness Prince Charles, Prince of Whales. Regular festival appearances include the Hollywood Bowl, Blossom, Wolf Trap, Saratoga, Flagstaff and Garden State. The Romeros are extremely popular with college audiences and make regular appearances on university series throughout the country as well as on the fine arts series of major cities. In New York they have appeared several times at Carnegie Hall, at Alice Tully Hall in Lincoln Center, at the Metropolitan Museum of Art's Grace Rainey Rogers Auditorium, at the Cloisters in upper Manhattan's Fort Tryon Park and on the Distinguished Artists Series at Rockefeller University. In addition to their extensive concertizing throughout the United States, they also regularly tour Europe and the Far East playing in every major city. Their 1987 tours of Europe and the Orient included more than forty concerts; virtually all of the performances were sold out, and one concert in Taipei was attended by over 10,000 people.

And I have a story. In latter days there was an opening and auditions for Director of the "Music in the Mountains" summer festival in Durango, Colorado at the rehearsal venue, the Purgatory Tent. Keah and I were avid fans of the festival since at least the second or third year in 1988. Mitsha Semanitsky (Russian, son of a cleric) was founder and director, from the Dallas Symphony. So, candidates came for the audition. Ángel Romero was one, and his performance would be the classic "Concierto de Aranjuez" for solo guitar and orchestra. Tradition was that there would be a morning rehearsal up in the tent, the performance that night. The rehearsal was a command performance we never saw altered. Angel did not show up for the rehearsal. There was chatter and I do not know the complete story, whether unavoidable or as someone in the morning sparse audience murmured: "Spanish arrogance". But Ángel's absence created a first: someone in the orchestra, a guest conductor, a substitute, announced he had directed the "Concierto" with Ángel the artist many times. "Not to fear; he will be here, and it will be wonderful." However, the orchestra needed the rehearsal. Said conductor "took the part" of the guitar and hummed and humdedumed the entire piece! He did not miss a note. And never will we ever experience that again.

Footnote: Angel did arrive and play the concert that night, but he did not for whatever reason become the new conductor.

Back to ASU and Gammage days, some years later, after the Romeros, I chanced upon, hearing from someone, that Christopher Parkening was to be over at the school of music and give a master class to the thriving ASU Classic Guitar Program. I had heard of him, heard his performances on TV or recordings, he a modern, contemporary master. It was said that in time off the road he spent his days at his getaway place in Montana or Idaho and fly fished for trout! What more could one desire: classic guitar and trophy trout! I don't remember much what he played that day, but it was the only master class I ever attended. I remember the nails on his right hand. Which leads to a final story of this part of the Musical Odyssey.

I have written two books telling of adventures as a cultural speaker for Brazilian topics on the National Geographic Explorer Ship for Lindblad Expeditions. See www.currancordelconnection.com . On the first trip in 2013 marking the 125th Anniversary of National Geographic Magazine the guest premier speaker was Wade Davis, a truly amazing and talented intellectual, writer and speaker, in the top ranks of the Geographic Society. Google him for an amazing experience. The connection is that his wife who accompanied him on the trip is a classical guitarist herself, and we had moments to talk of guitars, rosewood, Christopher Parkening a friend of hers, and yes, care of the nails for proper classic technique! I have always suspected that my inability to achieve proper tone even on the DiGiorgio is due to improper nail care. I just couldn't do "the drill." Close, but no cigar.

A short but final anecdote from the Explorer. There was a ship guitar, a rather fine steel stringed acoustic guitar the Filipino staff guys played in their onboard performances. I borrowed it a time or two to play "las mañanitas" for birthday moments. I had always wished I could have brought my DiGiorgio onboard and could have done classic and some singing during idle moments at sea. Alas it did not happen. But on one trip we received news of the death of Merle Haggard, one of my country favorites. I decided to do a "homage" to Merle in the lounge; it was all announced and we had a good crowd. Friends, it was a DISASTER, one of the worst moments (and there were few) of the Music Odyssey.

I and maybe a cohort were scheduled to sing a medley of Merle's best. The crack pianist, a guest on board, was set to accompany. We were in front of microphones. I could hardly fret those very difficult steel strings, but there's more: we were standing; my lyric sheets of the tunes were far below on a cocktail table (there was no music stand). I could not see them, could not remember the words, and tried to "fake it." No dice. I was embarrassed (although some said I had a fine voice), chagrined, but most of all disappointed that this crowd who admired the Brazilian expertise never would know the way I could play and sing. By that I mean the DiGiorgio and nylon strings and many of the titles you have seen in previous pages. Sometimes life throws a curve ball, or worse, a knuckler.

Back to Arizona. Until retirement in 2002 and then professional playing in restaurants in Durango from 2004 to 2007, and subsequent church music and performance, the main music in all those years in Tempe and then Mesa (1986 on) was practice at home of classic and singing the old folk songs and country music.

And playing classic guitar for meditation at our various parishes of our Catholic churches. That's the next chapter.

8

THE CATHOLIC DAYS AND MY CONTRIBUTION MUSIC FOR MEDITATION ON THE CLASSIC GUITAR

The first such moment took place at Resurrection Parish in Tempe, Arizona, the pastor and administrator in chief was Father Philip Poirier. He's not the point here although he did baptize our only daughter Katie in 1977 followed by a wonderful party of all our friends at our first house on Palmcroft Drive in Tempe.

Keah and I were both members of the decent church choir. The lead singer was a professional sort, soprano, maybe with music connections to the renowned program at ASU. We got along great; she knew how to handle such things. I think perhaps she was hired to sing; I don't know. I was invited to play some meditation music at some time, don't recall, before or during mass. It was then that genial, rotund Choir Director and Organist, Edgar Cook, invited me to play one piece, one of the classic Bach Fugues I think, at his "upper end" north Scottsdale Home Church. It was a concert situation; I was so nervous, the hands and the fingers never did loosen up, and I probably played a 65 per cent version. I was truly upset; Edgar understood, but that was that. I did continue at Resurrection until there was a move to nearby Holy Spirit Parish in Tempe. Keah and I were on the fringe of the move, but most of our close friends were leaving, so we did to. End of story.

The second such moment, and perhaps one which happened only once or twice, was when I played quiet classic music as a background to the communal confession service at Holy Spirit Church in Tempe, Arizona about 1985. It went well and folks said it indeed helped them to "quiet" their souls! The Pastor was the Reverend Mike O'Grady, perhaps only one of two or three Catholic Priests I have ever connected with. It's simple: I shared my beginning doubts as to the faith; he said, "Just come to the quiet church, sit a while and let whatever happens, happen." (Shades of the lyrics of Josh Groban's "You Raise me Up" of many years later, but perhaps no coincidence that the Catholic O'Grady knew of the old Irish folk hymn.)

One such musical moment was that St. Patrick's Day at Holy Spirit was the closest this Irish American ever came or felt close to his roots. (Other than well-oiled brother Jim singing "I'll Take You Home Again Kathleen" at weddings.) There was Irish step dancing by the nun, sister of Father Mike, and the two fathers did a hilarious rendition of "You're drunk, you're drunk, you silly old fool, you're drunk as drunk can be."

Father O'Grady I am convinced was a "straight – shooter" and after retiring as pastor of the Bishop's Church, St. Simon and Jude in downtown Phoenix, he became involved with "mini-retreats" of one night and a fervent task of raising money for the poor parishes of Peru.

A final footnote. Not being a native of Phoenix or privy to any serious history I was told that perhaps in the mid-1950s someone, a bishop perhaps, arranged for a whole slew of Irish seminarians soon to be priests to come to the wild and wooly west of Arizona. Such men were assigned to the burgs in the hinterlands, perhaps the mining areas, but eventually came to rule the Catholic Roost in Phoenix, being called the "Irish Mafia" by some.

Modern days have brought the horrific scandal of the Church and abuse in Ireland, of the young boys who served as altar boys, of young seminarians, and yes, of young women by priests and nuns alike. Ireland, they say, is getting over it and moving on with life. I might mention that the old Msgr. Roach of growing up days in Abilene, Kansas, was certainly an example of the Irish missionary priest.

Read "The Farm" where I talk all about it.

The final moment of this part of the Music Odyssey took place at St. Timothy's parish in Dobson Ranch in Mesa, this in 1986 when we purchased our second house on Cottonwood in Dobson Ranch, moving from the wonderful but modest first house in 1973 on Palmcroft in Tempe. This was an era when daughter Katie was growing up, participating in the church's religious programs. Yours truly donned coat and tie and lectored on Sundays in the vast church. Keah was the supportive foundation for our faith.

This was a very upscale Catholic Church, modern in architecture, built in the round, auditorium style. Pastors came and went, but the height of those days was Father Dale Fusek, certainly on track to be a bishop or more. He was instrumental in the organizing of hosting Pope John Paul II at ASU's football stadium in front of 70,000 fervent Catholics. He later did the same in hosting no less than Mother Teresa in her only visit to Arizona. The word was he arranged with financial wizard Charles Keating to borrow the company jet to fly her in. That is only hearsay. He was the diocese's best fund raiser in spite of the fact St. Timothy's was in a very middle-class area. His forté was liturgy with sermons that packed the church. (I recall "The Sermon on the Amount" once a year.) And a part of the outstanding liturgy was the music. He had dollars and wanted to make it worthwhile to his musicians, so he had the best:

THE INCREDIBLE CATHOLIC CONTEMPORTARY MUSIC OF TOM BOOTH, TIM AND JULIE SMITH, MATT MAHER AND GUESTS JON MICHAEL TALBOT AND KATHY TROCCOLI.

One looked forward to Sunday mass knowing that the upbeat choir would always inspire us, always with newly composed music. It truly was a golden age of Catholic music. All these folks were at one time on the NATIONAL scene in composition and performance.

It was in those latter years after being allowed by music director Tim Smith to copy any hymn I wanted from their vast library, and I had begun to learn to sing some of those songs as well, that I asked if I could perform "quiet music" during the week at mass. They gave me a trial and it went well. But then came THE MISTAKE. It was liturgical. On one such occasion, me thinking it really was going well, I was cornered after mass when told that my singing of "Hallelujahs" by Kathy Troccoli was sadly out of order – it was Lent and so no happy music!

I do not know if they never asked me back or what. But then came the event:

Father Dale was accused of shenanigans (never made totally public). This all is another story, but all that music would not have happened without him. And after his departure, St. Timothy's was indeed never the same. For sure, there was no music participation on my part. That would all come during our summers in Colorado, living at Vallecito Lake, being active parishioners at St. Bartholomew's in Bayfield, the next chapter in the Music Odyssey, albeit religious music.

9

Classic Guitar for Meditation
Singing Contemporary
Catholic
Accompanying Daughter Katie
St. Bartholomew's Bayfield Co

Music for Meditation, Mark, St. Bartholomew's

The classic guitar for meditation did find a home at our summer residence in Colorado and its mission parish, St. Bartholomew's of Bayfield. Due to the encouragement of our music director Therese Labree in approximately 1978, I began playing classical selections before mass, from about 8:00 to 8:25 each and every Sunday through the summer. From the very beginning I always prayed to myself, prior to starting the music, remembering the Jesuit motto AMDG (Ad Mayorem Dei Gloriam - To the Greater Glory of God) and tried to make the music my prayer. As mentioned, this began about in 1978 and continued for at least 20 years. It ceased only because the Knights of Columbus in the late 1990s or early 2000s decided we needed to say the Rosary before Mass each Sunday. You can't argue with the Blessed Virgin Mary, right?

Sometime during those middle 1990s daughter Katie, trained in classical violin, played just a few times and the photo shows our joint effort, me in this case just playing chord accompaniment to her solos. The theme from Schindler's List was heard in the environs of St. Barts!

Mark and Katie at St. Bartholomew's

As both choir directors and priest-pastors came and went over the years, the music contribution never went away, it just changed. Instrumental over many years was choir director Joan Reese who encouraged me to not only play just a bit before mass after the Rosary, but to sing those St. Timothy - era Catholic contemporary songs from Tom Booth, Tim and Julie Smith, Jon Michael Talbot, and Kathy Troccoli, perhaps on those days three pieces: one before mass, one at the Offertory and one at Communion, a meditation. Those were great years, most people really liked it, and it was good for my faith.

Now in recent years, things have changed, but I try to play three times during the summer or fall, once each month. Aside from the classical pieces already appearing in this narration, I might sing any of 52 selections learned over the years, a few favorites:

THE ST. TIMOTHY, ST. BART'S SONG LIST

1. Be with me Lord
2. Be not afraid
3. Forever will I sing

4. Give thanks to the Lord
5. Hail Mary, Gentle Woman
6. Hallelujahs
7. Here I am
8. Shepherd me o God
9. Holy is his name
10. How great thou are
11. I am the bread of life
12. I rejoiced when I heard them say
13. I will choose Christ
14. In the light of the Lord
15. Like a Deer
16. May I be his love
17. More than gold
18. One bread, one body
19. My Lady
20. Praise the Lord my soul
21. Resucitó
22. This shall be our prayer
23. City of God
24. Jerusalem my destiny
25. Come worship the Lord
26. Fullness of Life
27. Pachelbel. Make us a Eucharistic People
28. I am the vine
29. Healer of my soul
30. Breathe
31. Preghiera
32. You raise me up
33. Con te partiro'

10

RETIREMENT, THE MANUEL
RODRÍGUEZ CLASSIC GUITAR
A HIATUS FROM/ WITH ST.
BARTHOLOMEW'S
A RETURN TO PERFORMANCE IN
DURANGO, COLORADO 2004 -2007

The Retirement Music System

When I retired officially in 2002 from ASU, the cliché of a new red Corvette convertible was not the choice; it was something more important. I purchased a Manuel Rodríguez Electrified Classic Guitar from Milano's Music Store in Mesa Arizona, the guitar a fine East Indian Rosewood classic made in Madrid. But in addition there was a medium sized Fender amplifiyer, a microphone and a gadget I had run across up at Virginia's Steakhouse bar at Vallecito played by an itinerant musician who lived in his van (shades of Saturday Night Live and the comedian "motivational speaker" Chris who "lived in a van down by the river"). It was called a Vocal Harmonizer, invented I understood by the Mormons up in Salt Lake. You sing into the mike connected to the harmonizer and can get three, I said three, harmonized voices! Two would be enough to do the Everly Brothers! My aim at the time was to return to some kind of performing, but had no idea where. I recall this "call" to music was on my mind as I left the last unimpressive research meeting in Brazil in 2002. I was looking forward to retirement and Colorado.

A. THE FIRST "GIG" AT THE ITALIAN RESTAURANT

It had to be before that date, perhaps much before. Maybe through someone at church, a nice Italian girl who with her husband (a stern, serious Italian) had a restaurant on the upper level of the old Durango Mall on Main Avenue, it being way in the back and upstairs in the corner. Somehow we agreed that I would play one night in exchange for a meal. I think Keah was there. I played a lot of classic on the DiGiorgio and sang some folk songs and many by John Denver. No microphone, no amp, nada. It went well.

My mistake may have been to order the most expensive item on the menu, Shrimp Tempura, for the pay. I dunno. Only one other memory: of the very few people in the restaurant that night was a couple and he was a budding opera singer at Santa Fe and sang a few a capella songs. Such company we kept. Just the one night it was.

A footnote: in The Guitars – A Music Odyssey John Denver has to come into play. Both Keah and I loved him, and most Americans did at one time. "Take Me Home Country Road," "Rocky Mountain High" and the rest. We saw John at the height of his career sing and play to a sold-out ASU basketball arena crowd, perhaps 14,000 in attendance. The musicians' group was large, maybe 14 people with singers, all kinds of wonderful musicians, I remember the flautist. And standing ovations. This was probably in the late 1970s. The performance was repeated a year or two later, same crowd, same success.

But the eye-opener denouement took place at ASU's Sun City West a few years later. John Denver is in town, let's go! It was the venue for retirement crowds. John played and sang, there was a second instrumentalist, maybe guitar, a drummer and perhaps one other musician. He played the old songs and some new, but it was a weak version of the other concerts. It was sad, and we walked away sad. My main thought: this group seemed jaded like a side music show in a lounge in Las Vegas. We had followed John's huge success on television with the annual specials, then a documentary trip down the Grand Canyon in his comeback days, with new tunes, and overcoming a divorce and the alcohol problems. Then came the disaster of the small experimental aircraft on the Pacific coast. But as the song did not say, "The music did not die."

B. THE BIGGER RETIREMENT MOMENTS.

I had purchased the Manuel Rodríguez in 2002 as described, but had other fish to fry that first year with a summer teaching class in the "Getaway Program" at Fort Lewis College in Durango, a story I've told elsewhere. It all ended abruptly with the major wildfire that year when we were all evacuated from Vallecito. In retrospect, my fuzzy idea of part – time teaching during retirement at Fort Lewis never came to fruition, and it was for the best. A long drive into town. I supplanted that with years of wonderful classes and lectures at the Bayfield Public Library, always ending with the guitar and a music night.

The real music story was from 2004 to 2007 summers, a true return to performance. A lengthy story.

C. "BEATING THE BUSH" IN 2004

In the summer of 2004 I was itching and ready to return to a restaurant-bar to do the music. I made up a home-made professional card and hit the pavement in Durango. One likely place was the Citrus Café up on second avenue, but no dice.

D. THE PALACE RESTAURANT IN DURANGO

I did do one "gig," a one-nighter in the bar-lounge of the Palace Restaurant opposite the Durango-Silverton train station. This was a classy place, really beautiful inside with all the dark wood paneling, and the right crowd (I thought). Once again it was Mark and the DiGiorgio, no amp, no microphone, sitting in the corner of the lounge and playing classic, John Denver, some folk and probably some country. It went well and my reward was a nice dinner for Keah, Katie and me in the restaurant. Footnote: years later when I inquired about playing again, I was asked if I had tapes or CDs of my music. Alas!

E. WITS END RANCH RESTAURANT.

The next one-nighter was at the restaurant for the Wits End Ranch above Vallecito Lake back in its heyday. A bit of history: the ranch owner had gone into Durango on Main Street to the Crystal Tavern lounge and purchased all of their fine tall crystal glass mirrors originally from London; he moved them all to the bar at Wits End. The goal was to have fine décor for his fine dining. So I set up in the restaurant, played the standard tunes via the Manuel Rodríguez and vocal harmonizer and all. The owner told me later that it was "too loud." Hmm. In all honesty my system is nothing loud compared to the standard musicians today with big amps, maybe more than one. Anyway, that was that. I thought it had gone well. The owner ending selling all that prime beautiful real estate and scenery breaking it all up for condos. But the scenario was beautiful. Daughter Katie began her work career doing dishes in the kitchen and clean up, coming home smelling of strong kitchen cleanser. She later eventually moved up to waitress and enjoyed social life with all the young staff.

F. THE PURA VIDA CAFÉ.

A final one nighter and memorable at that. I played one night at the bar-restaurant of Pura Vida on the lake for Gary Peach owner and chef. A perfect location, 10 minutes up the road from our cabin. All went exceedingly well and I especially received compliments for the classical guitar selections. An aside: one of those incredible thunderstorms took place in late afternoon on the lake and patrons came in soaking wet, the girls' hair dripping with rain. Gary wanted someone steady and I only wanted once a month, so that was that. In later years a famous local entertainer, Greg Ryder, performed regularly once or twice a week; huge, big bass voice, good on the guitar, old country standards plus he wrote a lot of his own stuff.

Might as well say it now: I did/do not have one iota of song-writing blood in me, never wrote one, never tried to write one, never wanted to write one. But I could play the best of the famous folks. Just see the list.

G. THE BEST FOR LAST. CRISTINA'S BAR-RESTAURANT IN DURANGO

That leaves the best for last, my on-going relationship with Cristina's Café – Bar, first way north on Main in Durango, and then west on 160 across the Animas and a bit west. I would play at Cristina's once a month in the summer for four years until what I know and call "burn out."

Mark Playing at Cristina's

It all started at the old place on north Main. It was a bit dingy with a huge stage up in front where the bands played, in my case just me, the guitar, vocalizer, mike and amp. I recall tables out in front with a few customers, a huge big burning fireplace, and a bar way in front where several regulars gathered to drink boisterously and gamble. But the barkeep, a graduate from Fort Lewis and originally I think a ski enthusiast from Vermont who had enrolled at Fort Lewis College, gave me a terrific future tip for my music: "Check out 'O Brother Where Art Thou?' It's your kind of music." I did and spent a good part of the next winter learning all the tunes which would become a standard "set" in future work.

That following summer Cristina's moved to west of the river, was much nicer and brighter inside with great food, and when it was not raining in the summer, a nice outdoor patio venue where I played many times. Once or twice there was a big crowd all from St. Bart's parish, all our good friends. That was probably the best night, especially since they seemed to know many of the songs, including the Irish.

I would leave the cabin about 4:30 p.m., do the drive to Durango, take at least 30 minutes to unload all my stuff and set up (all the wires, amp, etc.) Play until about 9:00 p.m., take 30 minutes to pack up. Go inside and get my delicious dinner and two Ska Pin Stripe beers, and drive home in what seemed a very long drive.

One time I accidentally "trumped" Greg Ryder the local bass phenom. He was to play outside, me inside, it rained and I offered to give up my spot. The old pro probably didn't mind a night off and graciously ceded to me. Folks, he was **BIG TIME** in Durango; me the very small fish in the small pond. He was the guy who also played out at Pura Vida. A tragic end to his still vibrant life: driving into Durango from his home (I surmise in Hermosa) he was hit head on in early morning and was killed. We all lamented it and still miss him.

In those four years I must have added close to 200 songs to the repertoire. Most were learned in the wintertime in Mesa.

THE SONG LISTS – CRISTINA'S

I'm including the entire list of titles with this idea: each song for many of us is a memory in itself! They were all done in different sets.

The Classic Old Cowboy, Western and Country

1. Back in the Saddle Again. Gene Autry
2. High Noon. Tex Ritter
3. Streets of Laredo. Tex Ritter
4. Cool, Cool Water. Sons of the Pioneers.
5. The Cattle Call. Eddie Arnold
6. Ghost Riders in the Sky. Sons of the Pioneers
7. Red River Valley. Traditional

8. Strawberry Roam. Traditional/ Marty Robbins
9. San Antonio Rose. Bob Wills
10. Sixteen Tons. Tennessee Ernie Ford
11. The Yellow Rose of Texas. Traditional
12. Wabash Cannonball. Traditional
13. Mom and Dad's Waltz. Ernest Tubb
14. Movin' On. Hank Snow.

Then ... Country Classics

Patsy Cline
I fall to pieces
Crazy
Hank Williams
I can't help it if I'm still in love with you
Hear that lonesome whipporwill
Take these chains
There'll be no tears
You win again
Your cold, cold heart
Johnny Cash
I walk the line
Folsom Prison Blues
Grey Stone Chapel
Marty Robbins
El Paso
A White Sport Coat and a Pink Carnation
Jim Reeves
He'll have to go
Four Walls
Merle Haggard
Today I started loving you again

Silver Wings
Swingin' Doors
Oakie from Muskogee
Wanted Fugitive
Mama Tried
White Line Fever
Sing me back home
Willie Nelson
Blue eyes cryin' in the rain
On the road again
Georgia on my mind
Pancho and Lefty (with Merle Haggard)
My heroes have always been cowboys
Waylon Jennings
Don't let your babies grow up to be cowboys
Lukenbach Texas
Randy Travis
1982
On the other hand
My love is deeper
Forever and ever, Amen
Hard rock bottom of my heart
Kenny Rogers
Country Bumpkin
The coward of the county
The gambler
Lucille
Charlie Pride
The easy part's over now
But that was before I met you
The snakes crawl at night
Let the chips fall

Ray Price
For the good times
Sonny James
Young Love
The Gatlin Brothers – All the gold in California
Don Williams: Amanda
Alabama – My Home's in Alabama
Tanya Tucker – Delta Dawn, Queen of the Silver Dollar
John Connally – Rose colored glasses
Johnny Horton – the Battle of New Orleans
Miscellaneous old others:
Fraulein
I ain't never
I'll always remember
Making believe
Me and Bobby Mcgee
Oh lonesome me
Please help me I'm falling in love with you
Saginaw Michigan
Wayward wind
This peaceful sod
The Three Bells
Waterloo
Mark's favorites and train songs:
Folsom Prison Blues, The City of New Orleans, and St. James Infirmary Blues

COUNTRY CROSSOVER – JOHN DENVER

Poems, prayers and promises
Annie's Song
Back Home again

Country roads
Follow me
Leaving on a Jet Plane
Matthew
Rhymes and Reason
Rocky Mountain High
Sunshine on my shoulders
Perhaps love
Shanghai Breezes
Wild Montana Skies
Diamonds and Stones
This old guitar

TRADITIONAL FOLK (THE LIST ALREADY SEEN IN THE 50-50 CLUB CHAPTER)

EARLY POP AND ROCK N' ROLL

All I have to do is dream
Bye bye love
Poor little fool
That'll be the day
All shook up
Blue Suede Shoes
Hound Dog
Don't be cruel
Jailhouse Rock
Heartbreak Hotel
Blueberry Hill
Kansas City
Unchained Melody
San Francisco
Yesterday

The last farewell
Granma's lye soap
Summertime
Bebopalola
Standin' on the Corner
I was takin' a bath on a Saturday night – Young blood
Gonna rock it up

THE MEXICAN AND BRAZILIAN SET

SONGS IN SPANISH

20. Ya es muy tarde
21. Peregrina
22. Las mañanitas
23. Malagueña salerosa
24. Allá en el rancho grande
25. Coplas (canción chistosa de doble sentido)
26. Guantanamera
27. Adelita
    (Later, In retirement, for information only for Christina's in Durango, learned from Linda Ronstadt's "Canciones de mi padre")
28. El adiós del soldado
29. Jalisco
30. La Llorona
31. La Barca de Guaymas
32. Granito de Sal
33. Hay unos ojos
34. Y ándale

FOR INFORMATION ONLY, BRAZILIAN SONGS

35. Mulher rendeira
36. O vento

37. O canoeiro
38. Manhã de Carnaval

THE IRISH

1. If you're Irish, come into the parlour
2. Bold O'Donohue
3. Wild rover (parody)
4. Cockles and mussels
5. Loch Lomund
6. When Irish eyes are sSmiling (Galway Bay) (Those far away places)
7. Irish rover
8. Brennan on the moor
9. Wild colonial boy
10. Muirsheen Durkin
11. Danny Boy
12. The Rose of Tralee
13. My mother's hand
14. Gilgarry Mountain
15. The Holy Ground
16. I'll tell me Ma
17. I wish I was a maid again
18. Maids when you are young, never court an old man
19. Old maids in a garrett
20. Fiddler's green
21. Rosin the Bow
22. Maggie – O
23. Black Velvet Band
24. County of Armaugh
25. Irish lullaby
26. I'll take you home again Kathleen
27. It's a long way to Tipperary

28. Far side of the hill
29. When I first came to this land
30. The little land
31. Killarney
32. Green, green grass of home
33. McNamara's band
34. Galway Bay (parody)
35. Wearing of the green
36. Wild rover
37. Jug of punch
38. Dicey Reilley
39. Whiskey you're the devil
40. Have another drink boys
41. I've been a moonshiner
42. Who threw the overalls in Mrs. Murphy's chowder?
43. The night Paddy Murphy died
44. The old bog road
45. Spanish lady
46. Star of the County Down
47. Red is the rose
48. Mairi's wedding
49. Clancy lowered the boom
50. Seven drunken nights
51. She moved through the fair
52. The parting glass

THE "OH BROTHER WHERE ART THOU?" MEDLEY

1. You are my sunshine
2. Down to the river to pray
3. I am a man of constant sorrow
4. Don't leave nobody but the baby

5. Keep on the sunny side
6. I am weary; let me rest
7. I'll fly away
8. I'm in the jailhouse now
9. Angel band
10. Oh, Death

And while I'm at it, the great songs from Trio I and II with Emmy Lou Harris, Linda Ronstadt and Dolly Parton:

1. The pain of loving you
2. Those memories of you
3. Rosewood casket
4. Making plans
5. High Sierra
6. Wild flowers
7. My dear companion
8. Farther along
9. Lovers' return
10. Do I ever cross your mind?
11. Feels like home
12. When we're long, long gone.

I did all these songs, to be sure not on the same night, maybe not even in the entire season. I would do sets: old country, classic country, Oh Brother, John Denver, the Irish, the Spanish, and Classic. The melodies were in my head and all I needed to know was the key and maybe some accidental chords. But **I HAD TO HAVE** the lyrics in front of me all in plasticized sheets in big albums. So it was.

FINAL THOUGHTS AND EPILOGUE

So, there you have it. The entire story. Music at St. Bartholomew's still goes on sporadically. The most important thing remaining is the desire to practice and play music at home, not every day, but most days. I do a 45-minute memorized "set" of classical guitar selections and sing four favorites after that. On an energetic day I might try the old Flamenco. When inspired there is a return to serious study of famous classic guitar pieces. And I have a thick file folder I get out occasionally, with about 50 songs from the lists played at Cristina's. Most important is this: if I can imagine a concert of classical guitar music, me playing what I practice, that seems to keep it going. A concert fantasy.

ABOUT THE AUTHOR

Mark Curran is a retired professor from Arizona State University where he worked from 1968 to 2011. He taught Spanish and Portuguese and their respective cultures. His research specialty was Brazil and its "popular literature in verse" or the "Literatura de Cordel," and he has published many articles in research reviews and now some fourteen books related to the "Cordel" in Brazil, the United States and Spain.

Other books done during retirement are of either an autobiographic nature – "The Farm" or "Coming of Age with the Jesuits" - or reflect classes taught at ASU on Luso-Brazilian Civilization, Latin American Civilization or Spanish Civilization. The latter are in the series "Stories I Told My Students:" books on Brazil, Colombia, Guatemala, Mexico, Portugal and Spain. "Letters from Brazil I, II, III and IV" is an experiment combining reporting and fiction. "A Professor Takes to the Sea I and II" is a chronicle of a retirement adventure with Lindblad Expeditions - National Geographic Explorer. "Rural Odyssey – Living Can Be Dangerous" is "The Farm" largely made fiction. "A Rural Odyssey II – Abilene – Digging Deeper" and "Rural Odyssey III Dreams Fulfilled and Back to Abilene" are a continuation of "Rural Odyssey." "Around Brazil on the 'International Traveler' – A Fictional Panegyric" tells of an expedition in better and happier times in Brazil, but now in fiction. The author presents a continued expedition in fiction "Pre – Columbian Mexico – Plans, Pitfalls and Perils." Yet another is "Portugal and Spain on the 'International Adventurer.'" "The Collection" is a summary of primary and secondary works on the "Literatura de Cordel" in Curran's collection. A return to academic research and work was "The Master of the 'Literatura de Cordel' - Leandro Gomes de Barros - A Bilingual Anthology of Selected Works." Next is a return to the series of books dealing with research trips via Adventure Travel, a fictional account of "Adventure Travel in Guatemala – The Research Trip." And now an autobiographical volume in two parts: "Two by Mark J. Curran" Book I: ASU Days. Book II: The Guitars and a Music Odyssey.

Published Books

A Literatura de Cordel. Brasil. 1973

Jorge Amado e a Literatura de Cordel. Brasil. 1981

A Presença de Rodolfo Coelho Cavalcante na Moderna Literatura de Cordel. Brasil. 1987

La Literatura de Cordel – Antología Bilingüe – Español y Portugués. España. 1990

Cuíca de Santo Amaro Poeta-Repórter da Bahia. Brasil. 1991

História do Brasil em Cordel. Brasil. 1998

Cuíca de Santo Amaro – Controvérsia no Cordel. Brasil. 2000

Brazil's Folk-Popular Poetry – "a Literatura de Cordel" – a Bilingual Anthology in English and Portuguese. USA. 2010

The Farm – Growing Up in Abilene, Kansas, in the 1940s and the 1950s. USA. 2010

Retrato do Brasil em Cordel. Brasil. 2011

Coming of Age with the Jesuits. USA. 2012

Peripécias de um Pesquisador "Gringo" no Brasil nos Anos 1960 ou A Cata de Cordel" USA. 2012

Adventures of a 'Gringo' Researcher in Brazil in the 1960s or In Search of Cordel. USA. 2012

A Trip to Colombia – Highlights of Its Spanish Colonial Heritage. USA. 2013

Travel, Research and Teaching in Guatemala and Mexico – In Quest of the Pre-Columbian Heritage

> Volume I – Guatemala. 2013
> Volume II – Mexico. USA. 2013

A Portrait of Brazil in the Twentieth Century – The Universe of the "Literatura de Cordel." USA. 2013

Fifty Years of Research on Brazil – A Photographic Journey. USA. 2013

Relembrando - A Velha Literatura de Cordel e a Voz dos Poetas. USA. 2014

Aconteceu no Brasil – Crônicas de um Pesquisador Norte Americano no Brasil II, USA. 2015

It Happened in Brazil – Chronicles of a North American Researcher in Brazil II. USA, 2015

Diário de um Pesquisador Norte-Americano no Brasil III. USA, 2016

Diary of a North American Researcher in Brazil III. USA, 2016

Letters from Brazil. A Cultural-Historical Narrative Made Fiction. USA 2017.

A Professor Takes to the Sea – Learning the Ropes on the National Geographic Explorer.

Volume I, "Epic South America" 2013 USA, 2018.

Volume II, 2014 and "Atlantic Odyssey 108" 2016, USA, 2018

Letters from Brazil II – Research, Romance and Dark Days Ahead. USA, 2019.

A Rural Odyssey – Living Can Be Dangerous. USA, 2019.

Letters from Brazil III – From Glad Times to Sad Times. USA, 2019.

A Rural Odyssey II – Abilene – Digging Deeper. USA, 2020

Around Brazil on the "International Traveler" – A Fictional Panegyric, USA, 2020

Pre – Columbian Mexico – Plans Pitfalls and Perils, USA 2020

Portugal and Spain on the 'International Adventurer,' USA, 2021

Rural Odyssey III – Dreams Fulfilled and Báck to Abilene, USA, 2021

The Collection. USA, 2021

Letters from Brazil IV. USA, 2021.

The Master of the "Literatura de Cordel" – Leandro Gomes de Barros,2022

A Bilingual Anthology of Selected Works. USA, 2022

"Adventure Travel" in Guatemala – the Research Trip. USA, 2022

Two by Mark J. Curran. ASU Days and The Guitars – a Music Odyssey. USA, 2022

Professor Curran lives in Mesa, Arizona, and spends part of the year in Colorado. He is married to Keah Runshang Curran, and they have one daughter Kathleen who lives in Albuquerque, New Mexico, married to teacher Courtney Hinman in 2018. Her documentary film "Greening the Revolution" was presented most recently in the Sonoma Film Festival in California, this after other festivals in Milan, Italy and New York City. Katie was named best female director in the Oaxaca Film Festival in Mexico.

The author's e-mail address is: profmark@asu.edu
His website address is: www.currancordelconnection.com

Printed in the United States
by Baker & Taylor Publisher Services